TEXTUAL ANALYSIS

TEXTUAL ANALYSIS:
A BEGINNER'S GUIDE

ALAN McKEE

SAGE Publications
London • Thousand Oaks • New Delhi

First published 2003

SAGE Publications Ltd
6 Bonhill Street
London EC2A 4PU

SAGE Publications Inc
2455 Teller Road
Thousand Oaks, California 91320

SAGE Publications India Pvt Ltd
32, M-Block Market
Greater Kailash – I
New Delhi 110 048

British Library Cataloguing in Publication data

A catalogue record for this book is available from the British Library

ISBN 0 7619 4992 5
ISBN 0 7619 4993 3 (pbk)

Library of Congress Control Number: 2002112799

Typeset by Mayhew Typesetting, Rhayader, Powys
Printed and bound in Great Britain by TJ International, Padstow, Cornwall

To John Hartley – who makes sense.
To Terry Pratchett – who makes me look like an amateur.
And to Marc – who makes martinis.

Contents

Acknowledgements

Lots of academic books start off with the claim that all failings in the logic and presentation of ideas in this book are entirely the fault of the author. It's even more true for a personal rant like this. But still, without colleagues to test ideas on the book wouldn't exist. So thanks to, first of all, John Hartley, whose universe of meaning makes so much sense to me. His work and his person are inspiring, and I hope that he finds this book makes sense to him. And to Mark Gibson, who is unreasonably informed and intelligent. Both provided invaluable feedback on early drafts of the book. To Julia Hall at Sage, who said, 'What a good idea', and then left me to it; and Jamilah Ahmed, who was intelligent and helpful in her feedback. To many colleagues who make thinking exciting: Catharine Lumby, Kath Albury, Kate Bowles, and the members of the *Continuum* editorial collective, all of whom have contributed to the ideas in this book in one way or another. A special mention for Tamara Bycroft, who saved me, at the last minute, from making a tit of myself. Thanks to everyone. I hope the book doesn't make them embarrassed to have their names mentioned in it.

What is textual analysis? 1

What is textual analysis?

Textual analysis is a way for researchers to gather information about how other human beings make sense of the world. It is a methodology – a data-gathering process – for those researchers who want to understand the ways in which members of various cultures and subcultures make sense of who they are, and of how they fit into the world in which they live. Textual analysis is useful for researchers working in cultural studies, media studies, in mass communication, and perhaps even in sociology and philosophy.

Let's open with a straightforward description

What is textual analysis?

When we perform textual analysis on a text, we make an educated guess at some of the most likely interpretations that might be made of that text.

We interpret texts (films, television programmes, magazines, advertisements, clothes, graffiti, and so on) in order to try and obtain a sense of the ways in which, in particular cultures at particular times, people make sense of the world around them. And, importantly, by seeing the variety of ways in which it is possible to interpret reality, we also understand our own cultures better because we can start to see the limitations and advantages of our own sense-making practices.

Is that the only way to study texts?

Of course, I'm trying to make things simple here, and nothing is really that simple. This book only introduces one version of textual analysis. Academics who do 'textual analysis' actually practise a huge range of methodologies – many of which are mutually contradictory and incompatible (for a sense of this range, see Allen, 1992). This book explains a form of 'textual analysis' whereby we attempt to understand the likely interpretations of texts made by people who consume them. This is not the only 'correct' methodology for gathering information about texts. Other approaches can also produce useful information: no approach tells us the 'truth' about a culture. It's important to realize that different methodologies will produce different kinds of information – even if they are used for analysing similar questions.

For example, suppose you were interested in what the responses of television viewers to an imported American programme (like the 1980s' soap opera *Dynasty*) have to tell us about how audiences make sense of the nation in which they live. You could try to find out this information in a number of ways. Professor Jostein Gripsrud includes two of these in his book *The Dynasty Years* (1995). On the one hand, Gripsrud draws on large-scale, numerical surveys about *Dynasty* viewers. He uses ratings information, for example, to tell us how many people watched the programme – finding out that in December 1988, 63 per cent of the women and 57 per cent of the men surveyed in his home country of Norway had seen at least one episode of *Dynasty* in the season that had just run. This is useful information – but it doesn't tell us anything about the *ways* in which viewers watch this programme. It doesn't tell us how they interpreted it, what they thought it was about, what relationship they thought it had to their own lives (Gripsrud, 1995: 113). Gripsrud goes on to investigate other issues in this large-scale survey, asking viewers what they disliked about the programme. He points out that less than 25 per cent of the people surveyed thought that the programme was 'unrealistic', for example. He uses this evidence to suggest that the viewers of the programme are likely to be relating it to their own life in some way (ibid.: 116).

But this methodology still doesn't produce any information about *how* these viewers might have been watching *Dynasty*. In order to produce large-scale, generalizable information, it is necessary to turn people into numbers. There's no other way to handle the information. So Gripsrud does this. He produces categories, and he fits people into them but this information doesn't give us any sense of how audience members actually use a programme. To produce that kind of information would require a different kind of approach, different kinds of questions – a quite different methodology.

Gripsrud quotes an interview with one viewer of *Dynasty*. The amount of detail and specificity about this one viewer is amazing compared with her status in the official ratings as a single unit:

> [This *Dynasty* fan] is an intelligent bank employee in her thirties . . . her husband has a bit more education but . . . far less intelligence . . . her husband regularly beats her and humiliates her in various other ways . . . When telling the interviewer about her sexual misery, the wife on her own initiative started talking about *Dynasty* 'You know, I'm quite romantic, you see . . . What I like to watch on television is *Dynasty* . . . I dream that I'd like some tenderness and compassion.' (ibid.: 156)

In the methodology of large-scale surveys, processed as numbers, such a viewer becomes, perhaps, 0.1 per cent of the people who don't think that *Dynasty* is 'unrealistic'. Using that methodology, the similarity of her position to that of other viewers is emphasized. But in an interview like this, it is the *uniqueness* of her situation that becomes obvious – the individual ways in which her own life experience informs the use she makes of this television programme, and the interpretations she produces of it.

These two different methodologies produce quite different pictures of television viewers and their interpretative practices. This is because the questions that you ask have an effect on the information that you find. Different methodologies produce different kinds of answers.

This is an important point. There isn't one true answer to the question of how viewers watch this television programme. Depending on how you gather your information, you will find different answers. And you can't just fit these different pieces of information together like a jigsaw to produce the 'truth' about how viewers watch *Dynasty*. You can know in detail how a small number of people watch a programme; or you can know in a more abstract way how lots of people watch. But you can't really know both at once. If we simply interviewed every one of the millions of Norwegian *Dynasty* viewers in this way, we still wouldn't end up with a perfectly accurate picture of how they *really* interpret this text. Quite apart from the inconceivable cost of such a project, at some point it would be necessary to boil down the information, to look for patterns, to reduce viewers' experiences to the things that they have in common, in order to produce an account that wasn't twenty million words long. As soon as the information is boiled down into categories, it presents a different type of picture to that which emerges from the individual interview – but no less of a true one. Different methodologies produce different kinds of information – they might not even be compatible.

What is a text?

If textual analysis involves analysing texts, then – what exactly is a text? Answer: whenever we produce an *interpretation* of something's *meaning* – a book, television programme, film, magazine, T-shirt or kilt, piece of furniture or ornament – we treat it as a text. A text is something that we make meaning from.

So why not just say 'book' or 'film' or whatever?

We use the word 'text' because it has particular implications. There are no two exact synonyms in the English language – words always have slightly different meanings and connotations. The word 'text' has post-structuralist implications for thinking about the production of meaning.

And that would mean, exactly . . .?

Different cultures make sense of the world in very different ways. Times Books International publishes a series of books to help travellers visiting other countries. The series is called 'Culture Shock' (Craig, 1979; Hur and Hur, 1993; Roces and Roces, 1985). The books are not just tourist guides: they are attempts to help the visitor – as their title suggests – overcome 'culture shock': the experience of visiting another culture that's different not only in language, but in its whole way of making sense of the world. In their book on the Philippines, Alfredo and Grace Roces use this example to explain how different another culture's ways of making sense of the world can be:

> After two years in the Philippines, Albert G Bradford, an American Peace Corps Volunteer wrote to one of his colleagues: 'I remember how quickly I discovered that people didn't understand me. The simplest things to me seemed not familiar to them at all. I tried to explain, but the further I got into an explanation, the sillier I looked; suddenly I felt undermined: the most basic premises, values and understandings were of no help to me . . . for these understandings and ways of doing and seeing things just didn't *exist* even. There was a big gap. (Roces and Roces, 1985: 83, emphasis in original)

Studying other cultures makes clear that, at many levels, the ways of making sense of the world employed can be quite different: 'The

Western visitor [to the Philippines] finds he is talking the same language, but not communicating at all . . . he [sic] is in an entirely different world' (ibid.: 1). These differences operate at a variety of levels, from the more superficial, to those which challenge our very foundations for thinking about what reality is and how it works.

Differences in value judgements

At the simplest level, cultures may ascribe different levels of value to things around them. For example, every culture includes people who have more body fat than others. But there is no universal agreement about whether having more body fat than your fellow citizens is a good thing or a bad thing. In Western countries a combination of medical and aesthetic discourses insist that being larger is not a good thing: it is neither attractive nor healthy, we are forever being told. We are constantly surrounded by reminders that this is the case, by people who might, for example, buy a T-shirt that says: 'No fat chicks' ('Enter a room/bar or event and let fat chicks know your [sic] not intrested [sic]', Shirtgod, 2002; luckily, you can avoid such people by wearing a T-shirt yourself that says: 'No morons who can't spell').

And such value judgements aren't natural, nor are they universal. In other cultures, completely different standards apply. In the African country of Niger, being larger is a positive quality and something to be sought after:

> Fat is the beauty ideal for women in Niger, especially in the village of Maradi where they take steroids to gain bulk, pills to sharpen appetites and even ingest feed or vitamins meant for animals; many compete to become heaviest and train for beauty contests by gorging on food. (Onishi, 2001: 4)

The idea that different cultures make different value judgements about things is common sense – we already know this. But the differences in sense making practices in various cultures go much further than this.

Differences in the existence of abstract things

In books about cross-cultural communication, you often find phrases like: 'it has not been possible to find satisfactory English translations for these expressions [of 'Hungarian politeness and greetings formulas and forms of address']' (Balazs, 1985: 163); or '[i]n the Hopi language . . . there is no word for "time"' (Fuglesang, 1982: 40).

Abstract nouns, describing things that don't have a physical existence, vary markedly from culture to culture. We can attempt to translate these from language to language, but these translations are often rough – trying to find the closest equivalents in a different sense-making system, but differing quite widely. 'Hiya' for example, is 'the foremost social value' in the Philippines, according to *Culture Shock*, and can be roughly translated as 'shame' but 'It is rather a difficult word to define', because the range and scope of this concept, and the variety of ways in which it functions in Filipino culture, have no equivalent in English:

> It is a universal social sanction, creating a deep emotional realisation of having failed to live up to the standards of society . . . Filipino employees tend not to ask questions of a supervisor even if they are not quite sure what they should do, because of hiya; a host may spend more than he can afford for a party, driven by hiya; an employee dismissed from his job may react violently because of hiya. (Roces and Roces, 1985: 30)

Some cultures have no words for 'round', 'square' or 'triangular' (Fuglesang, 1982: 16) – these concepts aren't useful for their way of life. Others don't have words for, and don't use the concepts of, abstractions like 'speed' or 'matter' (Whorf, quoted in Fuglesang, 1982: 34). The way in which they make sense of the world is not built on these abstractions that are so familiar to Western culture. Anthropologist Fuglesang describes the culture of Swahili speakers in Africa, and the ways in which they make sense of the world without the abstract nouns that Westerners are used to. For example, the answer to the question: 'How big is your house?' is 'I have house for my ancestors, the wife, and God gave me eight children, Bwana'. With repeated questioning, it turns out that the house is 'fifteen paces'. When asked, 'How long is a pace?', the answer is: 'The headman, Mr Viyambo, does the pacing in the village, Bwana' (quoted in Fuglesang, 1982: 34). In the Western world-view, such answers don't make sense. In Swahili, because measurement is not an abstract, the answer is meaningful – it tells the questioner all that they need to know about *how* this measurement was done. For the speaker, this is the really important thing. Similarly, the absence of an abstract 'time' leads to different ways of making sense of experience: 'When was your son born, Mulenga?'; 'My son was born two rainy seasons after the great drought' (ibid.: 1982: 37–8). As Fuglesang says, 'time only exists when it is experienced . . . In the African village . . . it is simply non-sensical to say "I do not have time"' (ibid.: 38).

Differences in the existence of concrete things

This is the difficult part. It's possible to argue that in different sense-making structures, even physical objects exist differently. The commonest example for this is the multiple words that Inuit languages have for describing snow, where English only has one. An Inuit speaker can describe, can distinguish between – can, in a way, *see* – many different kinds of object in a snowy landscape (different kinds of snow). An English speaker, who doesn't have the culture, knowledge or experience to distinguish between them, won't see many different kinds of object. For him or her, there is only undifferentiated 'snow'. The different kinds of snow don't exist for the English speaker as differentiated objects. This is not simply a different value judgement on elements of reality – it's seeing reality differently. Objects don't exist in the same way in the sense-making practices of different cultures. Objects – and even people – can be fitted into quite different categories in different ways of making sense of the world:

> in western societies there is a tripartite division of age groups into children, youngsters [adolescents] and adults – with an almost cultic social attention accorded to youth and the youthful, and conversely, a badly concealed contempt for old age. In other societies, for example, Bantu societies in Africa, the divisions have a different status emphasis and follow different lines – children, adults, elders. (Fuglesang, 1982: 77)

There is no equivalent of 'elder' in Western culture. Not all old people are elders; not all elders are old people. It is a different kind of person – a wise person with a high social standing because of their knowledge and experience – who doesn't exist in Western cultures.

Differences in relationships between things

Noting that it isn't possible to translate a number of Hungarian words that are 'politeness and greetings formulas and forms of address' into English, Balazs states that until the nineteenth century, Hungary had no general word for 'you' that didn't imply a social relationship of inferiority and superiority to the speaker – everyone had to establish such a relationship every time they spoke to each other. By contrast, in our modern English sense-making systems, we don't need to place each other into a position of inferiority or superiority when we speak to each other. Similarly, the linguist Benjamin Lee Whorf noted that in the Native American language 'Hopi' it is not even possible to say 'my room' – there's no phrase in the language that equates to this.

'Hopi society does not reveal any individual proprietership . . . of rooms' (Whorf, 1956: 201). So different sense-making systems demand, or allow, different ways of thinking about the relationships between people and things. In English, you *can* own a room.

Differences in reason and thinking

The way in which it's possible to construct an argument in Western culture is commonly based on logical reasoning systems that we inherit from classical Greece. These underlie our mathematical systems as well, and we often think of them as being the only correct way in which such reasoning can take place. After all, 2 + 2 = 4. But they are not the only correct forms of logic. As John D. Barrow, Professor of Astronomy at the University of Sussex, argues, Western sense-making works:

> [with] a two-valued logic . . . every statement has two possible truth values: it is either true or false . . . [but in] a non-Western culture like that of the Jains in ancient India, one finds a more sophisticated attitude towards the truth status of statements. The possibility that a statement might be indeterminate is admitted . . . Jainian logic admits seven categories for a statement . . . (1) maybe it is; (2) maybe it is not; (3) maybe it is, but it is not; (4) maybe it is indeterminate; (5) maybe it is, but it is indeterminate; (6) maybe it is not but is indeterminate; (7) maybe it is and it is not, and is also indeterminate . . . We [mathematicians] do not attach any character of . . . absolute truth to any particular system of logic . . . there exists more than one formal system whose use as a logic is feasible, and of these systems one may be more pleasing or more convenient than another, but it cannot be said that one is right and the other wrong. (Barrow, 1992: 15, 16)

Differences in seeing things

Perhaps the most surprising differences come in evidence that people living in different sense-making systems can literally see the world differently. A subdiscipline of psychology looking at visual perception has focused on optical illusions in order to try to understand how our brains process visual information. One of these is the so-called Müller-Lyer figure (two parallel horizontal lines of equal length; the top one has an arrow-head at each end pointing outwards, the bottom one has an arrow head at each end pointing inwards).

Most Europeans get taken in by this optical illusion, and think that the top line is shorter than the bottom line, even though they're both identical when measured with a ruler. But people from non-European cultures, it turns out, 'showed much less illusion effect' (Coren and Girgus, 1978: 140; Robinson, 1972: 109). Indigenous Australians, for example, were 'decidedly less susceptible to the illusion than were the British scientists administering the tests' (Froman, 1970: 52). In short, psychology argues that 'what a person sees is determined by what he guesses he sees' (ibid.: 59). People from different sense-making systems can literally see the world differently (Coren and Girgus, 1978: 141; Robinson, 1972: 110).

I can see that other cultures make sense of the world very differently but perhaps they are wrong, and my culture is correct?

True. If we accept that different cultures have different sense-making practices, and that they see reality in a variety of different ways, the next question is: how do we judge those different ways of making sense of the world?

I think there are basically three different responses to this question:

- A *realist* response: my culture has got it right. It simply describes reality. Other cultures are wrong.
- A *structuralist* response: all these cultures seem to be making sense of the world differently; but really, underneath, they have common structures. They're not all that different; people across the world are basically the same.
- A *post-structuralist* approach: all these cultures do indeed make sense of the world differently: and it is impossible to say that one is right and the others are wrong. In a sense, people from different cultures experience reality differently.[1]

All these positions exist in current Western cultures; and all have histories that we can trace back to previous centuries. Some nineteenth-century British anthropologists, for example, thought that the other cultures they studied were – as the title of a key book by Professor E.B. Tylor puts it – *Primitive Culture* (1871). They thought these cultures were a less evolved state of society, and studying them could: 'thro[w] light upon the earlier stages of culture of civilised peoples [i.e. British people]' (ibid.: 131). These anthropologists thought that their own culture – their sense-making practices – simply described how the world really was. Other cultures were interesting, but we couldn't learn from them how to think differently. The anthropologists studied them, in a sense, because they were fascinated by just how wrong they were. This is what I call a 'realist' way of thinking about the difference between cultures: thinking that one way of representing and making sense of reality can be the true one; so all others are necessarily wrong.

Other anthropologists in the nineteenth century studied other cultures – and particularly their religions – so they could find out what they had in common. They tried to look beyond superficial differences to find underlying structures: 'the universal spirit which every creed tries to embody' (Haddon, 1910: 137). These anthropologists looked for common images in different religions – like the figure of a sun or a moon god – and then found them in religious texts of different cultures, even when they were not apparent to most observers. As one early account of this practice puts it: 'certain [anthropologists], such as Ehrenreich, Foy and Frobenius find the sun and moon gods in the most unlikely places' (ibid.: 142).

The third approach, what I call 'post-structuralism' (although that word is a recent label for it), can be traced back to the work of nineteenth-century philosophers like Friedrich Nietzsche. Nietzsche's work only really addressed previous philosophical writing, rather than cultures generally, but it is possible to trace a history that links his thinking to the kinds of cultural relativism that I'm describing here (Cuff et al., 1998: 239). He argued that Western culture (in particular, the place of 'reason' as the ultimate form of human thought and best way of organizing a society) was only one possible approach to sense-making, and not the ideal end point of human evolution. Rather than seeing rational descriptions of the world as simply describing the 'truth' of the world, 'post-structuralist' approaches to sense-making see all forms of language – all sense-making strategies – as having their own advantages and limitations (ibid.: 242).

As I said above, all these positions still exist in Western cultures. And because the question is ultimately a philosophical one about the nature of reality and our relationship to it, it's not possible to prove which is correct. There's no irrefutable argument that you can make to prove one over the other.

The position that I'm taking in this book – the one that makes most sense to me – is the third one: the form of cultural relativism that I call post-structuralism. It seems to me that we make sense of the reality that we live in through our cultures, and that different cultures can have very different experiences of reality. No single representation of reality can be the *only* true one, or the *only* accurate one, or the *only* one that reflects reality because other cultures will always have alternative, and equally valid, ways of representing and making sense of that part of reality. As I say, I can't prove that this is correct. I think this way because of the kinds of information that I've mentioned above – about how very different the sense-making practices of other cultures are – and the fact that many of those cultures seem to function perfectly well even though their understanding of reality is very different from mine. It seems to me that it would be a bit of a coincidence if I just happened to be born into the only culture that's got it right. The reason that I think like this might also be due to some personal experience. I was a born-again Christian for many years, and did believe quite firmly that my way of making sense of the world was right, and everybody else's was wrong. When I stopped being a Christian, I started to be suspicious of people who claimed that their way of seeing the world was the only correct one.

It's worth noting that this kind of culturally relativist post-structuralism isn't just limited to academics who live in ivory towers and have nothing to do with the real world (to use some common insults that are often thrown at us – although I've never actually met an academic who lives in an ivory tower; and most of us still do our shopping in the real world). More and more people are travelling internationally, and business in particular is ever more transnational. This means that even those people who are concerned with making money, and so are often held up as the epitome of 'the real world' (that is, businesspeople) increasingly acknowledge cultural relativism as a necessary reality of their work. You do business with people who are human beings, people that you have to convince, persuade and seduce to work with you (although there is some overlap in international situations, business is slightly different from war – you can't just kill your potential partners if they don't submit). This is one reason that there has recently been a massive increase in research into 'cross-cultural communication' (Loveday, 1985: 31). An increasing number of manuals aimed at business people attempt to explain just how different the ways of making sense of the world of various cultures are (see, for example, Gannon and Newman, 2002; Hendon et al., 1996; Yamada, 1992). It is important for business to understand how colleagues in other cultures make sense of the world differently, accept those differences, and work with them. For an American businessperson visiting Japan, for example:

> At first, things in the cities look pretty much alike. There are taxis, hotels . . . Theatres . . . But pretty soon the American discovers that

underneath the familiar exterior there are vast differences. When someone says 'yes' it often doesn't mean yes at all, and when people smile it doesn't always mean they are pleased. When the American visitor makes a helpful gesture, he may be rebuffed; when he tries to be friendly, nothing happens. People tell him that they will do things and don't. The longer he stays, the more enigmatic the new country looks. (Hall, quoted in Adler, 1987: 25)

The physical surroundings may look similar, but the way in which the culture makes sense of them is very different. This is a post-structuralist position, taught to businesspeople as a necessary part of the very real concern of making money internationally. It's not possible to prove that this is the 'correct' way to understand the different ways that cultures interpret their realities,: but for me, and for these international businesspeople, it's one that makes sense.

This, then, is why I use the word 'text': as well as being a convenient term for all the various elements of culture that we use to produce interpretations (including, as suggested above, not just books, films, magazines and television programmes, but also clothing, furniture, and so on), this term has been favoured by post-structuralist writers. Using this word implies a post-structuralist approach to culture – trying to work out how cultures make sense of the world, not so we can judge them against our own culture, and not to seek out deep truths across cultures, but to map out and try to understand the variety of different ways in which peoples can make sense of the world.

It is also why we sometimes use the word 'read' instead of 'interpret' when we're talking about culture; rather than writing 'how do people interpret this text?', we use, 'how do people read this text?'. Even if it's a film or a television programme, we talk about 'reading' it. Again, the word has post-structuralist implications.

What's all this got to do with textual analysis?

Depending on what approach you take to judging different cultures' sense-making practices – the different ways they make sense of the world – you analyse texts in different ways. From a 'realist' perspective, you look for the single text that you think represents reality most accurately, and judge all other texts against that one. From a 'structuralist' perspective, you look for the deep structures that aren't actually apparent in the text, but that you can find by specialized

稻衣本之間二彳

training. From a 'post-structuralist' perspective, you look for the differences between texts without claiming that one of them is the only correct one.

Okay. Fine. I'm convinced. But most of the texts that I'm going to be analysing don't come from other cultures – they're produced in my own country, or in ones with very similar cultures – America, Britain, or Australia. So how relevant is all this?

Traditional anthropology was about studying exotic cultures the more different they were from Western culture, the more interesting they were (particularly indigenous African, American and Australian cultures). But in the course of the twentieth century anthropologists realized that they could study their own nations as well (Stocking, 1982: xiii). These kinds of studies made it clear that even within a single nation there exist a variety of different cultures. As Ralph Linton puts it in his 1936 introduction to anthropology: 'While [cultural anthropologists] have been accustomed to speak of . . . nationalities as though they were the primary culture-bearing units, the total culture of a society of this type is really an aggregate of sub-cultures' (1936: 275). That is to say, a national culture isn't made up of millions of identical people who all make sense of the world in exactly the same way. Rather, it consists of a mixture of many overlapping subcultures. For example, anthropologists have identi-fied distinct (sub)cultures – distinct groupings of people who make sense of the world in their own ways – organized around hobbies and lifestyle choices (Irwin, 1962); race (Kitano, 1969); geographical loca-tion (Morland, 1971); the kinds of work people do (Turner, 1971); age and cultural (music) preferences (Cohen, 1972); and sexuality (Wotherspoon, 1991), among other factors. And they found that these subcultures made sense of the world in many different ways. Not only their value judgements, but their abstract systems, logic and forms of reasoning could vary remarkably, even within one nation. As above, you can respond to this fact by dismissing other sub-cultures' sense-making practices as simply wrong compared to your own – a lot of early research called these subcultures 'deviant' (Irwin, 1962). But you can also believe that these subcultures may have quite valid different ways of making sense of the world. Many cross-cultural communication guides now include two different kinds of information: 'International' cross-cultural communication (*between* nations) and 'Intranational' cross-cultural communications (*within* nations) (see Brunt and Enninger, 1985); because: 'Communicative misunderstandings, conflicts and derailments can occur not only between national groups, but also between cultural groups within the same nation' (ibid.: 119). Researchers have argued that although the differences in sense-making between subcultures are not as vast as those between, for example, British and Swahili cultures, they are still real. And you have to take account of these differences if you want to communicate with people from different subcultures. As one cross-cultural guide puts it:

> When adults talk with their teenagers about the drug scene, the success of the discussion will depend greatly on the adults' ability to talk about drugs in a way that carries meaning in terms of adolescent concerns and experiences – and vice versa . . . The dictionary meaning is of limited use: 'A substance with medical, physiological effects'. This does not take into account the fact that adults and teenagers bring their own world of experience and association into the meaning of the word . . . The meaning of the word is determined in large part by each person's characteristic frame of reference. (Szalay and Fisher, 1987: 167)

Performing textual analysis, then, is an attempt to gather information about sense-making practices – not only in cultures radically different from our own, but also within our own nations. It allows us to see how similar or different the sense-making practices that different people use can be. And it is also possible that this can allow us to better understand the sense-making cultures in which we ourselves live by seeing their limitations, and possible alternatives to them.

Of course, if I pushed this thinking to its logical limit I could say that within British culture, there's a British youth culture; within that, a Black British youth culture; a Black male British youth culture; a straight Black male British youth culture; a Northern straight Black male British youth culture; and so on, until everybody would be reduced to their own culture, with a membership of one. This is true: but it shouldn't be a paralysing realization. All of us reach a broad consensus about sense-making practices within the variety of nested cultures in which we live. While it is ultimately true that nobody else sees everything about the world exactly the same way that we do, we overlap enough to live together, and to communicate with other. The consensus at the level of the largest communities – say, a national culture – is enough for us to make sense of it most of the time, but may often jar with our own practice: sometimes we'll hear people who share a nation with us saying things that just don't make any sense to us; we can't understand how they could possibly think that way. As the communities we are discussing become smaller and more specialized, it is likely that the sense-making consensus will fit our own practices more precisely.

You're writing a lot about 'sense-making practices' – but how can analysing texts help us to understand sense-making practices?

Texts are the material traces that are left of the practice of sense-making   the only empirical evidence we have of how other people make sense of the world. John Hartley uses the metaphor of forensic science to describe this process. Forensic scientists never actually see a crime committed – by the time they arrive on the scene, it has gone forever. They can never wind back time and witness it themselves; and they can never be entirely certain about what happened. But what they can do is sift through the evidence that is left – the forensic evidence – and make an educated and trained guess about what happened, based on that evidence. The fact that, unlike physics, this science is not repeatable – they can't murder people themselves to see if it turns out exactly the same – doesn't stop them, as scientists, using their training and expertise to attempt to build up a picture of what happened. This can stand as a metaphor for what we do when we perform textual analysis: we can never see, nor recover, the actual practice of sense-making. All that we have is the evidence that's left behind of that practice – the text: 'the material reality [of texts] allows for the recovery and critical interrogation of discursive politics in an "empirical" form; [texts] are neither scientific data nor historical documents but are, literally forensic evidence' (Hartley, 1992: 29).

As Hartley says, forensic science relies on 'clues'. This is how textual analysis also works. We can never know for certain how people interpreted a particular text but we can look at the clues, gather evidence about similar sense-making practices (see Chapter 5), and make educated guesses.

So we're not analysing texts to see how accurate they are in their representation of reality?

No, this form of post-structuralist textual analysis is not about measuring media texts to see how accurate they are. But, as I said above, this is only one methodology that can be used in cultural studies, media studies or mass communication studies. The 'realist' mode of analysing texts, described above, is still an important one within these disciplines. This is particularly the case in media studies, where many writers seek to measure texts against reality. Indeed, this is the most common public mode of thinking about media texts. It seems like common sense:

- Texts can be measured as being more or less *accurate*.
- Which is to say, they can be measured as to how accurately they tell *the truth*.
- Which is to say, they can be measured as to how accurately they tell the truth about *reality*. (see Ellis, 2000: 13)

The difficulty with this approach, from a post-structuralist perspective, is that these terms don't recognize that people might make sense of reality in quite different ways (as shown above). People tend to use these words in moralistic ways to insist that there's only one correct way of making sense of any situation, and it's *their* way of doing it; any other approach is not just an alternative – it is necessarily *wrong*.

Take the example of the Christian Minister interviewed on the current affairs programme *A Current Affair* on the 7 November 2001. The debate is about whether children should be caned in school? A 'Parents and Citizens' group is arguing that the law should stand as it is – children shouldn't be caned. They present their reasons and their arguments for this approach. The Minister is then interviewed. He says: 'I can't think of any group of people who are less in touch with reality than the P[arents] and C[itizens].'

Is he right? Do these people have no contact with reality? Are they all quite, quite mad? Of course, what he means is that he disagrees with them. They make sense of the behaviour of children, the role of schooling, and what would make a desirable society in ways that are so bizarre to him that the only possible explanation is that these people have no grasp on reality. And reality is . . . the way that he sees the world. When the interviewer suggests that: 'That's not a very nice thing to say. You're meant to be a Christian', the Minister replies. 'It's the truth. Being a Christian is about telling the truth.' This is 'the truth'. The position put by those who see the world differently from him is obviously not 'the truth'. Their description of the situation, their interpretation of how it should be dealt with, is not the truth. It may be lies; it may be madness; but it is not the truth. What is the truth? The truth is the Minister's perspective (for other examples of this common tendency, see Bantick, 2001: 13; McGrory and Lister, 2001: 7; Pullan, 1986: 153).

Another term which often gets pulled into these realist forms of textual analysis is 'bias' – a word that's used to claim that a text is not accurate. But as Blain Ellis points out: 'When complaints of bias are received . . . [p]roducers recognize that most charges are made in terms of people's own subjective bias'. He provides one of my favourite statistics: 'Of all complaints of bias [in television coverage] received after the 1975 elections, 412 said the [Australian Broadcasting Corporation] favoured Labor and 399 said it favoured the coalition parties [the two major sides in the election]' (Ellis, 1977: 89). We tend to think that the terms 'truth' and 'reality' are simple, straightforward and obvious. We assume, without ever really thinking about it, that there is only one possible truth about any given situation; or that everyone agrees on what the 'reality' of that situation is. But in practice (in the real world) if you look at how people use the word 'truth' in their public discussions, you see that they in fact use it to mean 'what my community thinks'. It's a moral term: we use it to make a claim about how people *should* think. It doesn't really matter if people disagree with an *opinion* that we have – it's just an opinion, after all. But if they disagree with something that we think is 'the truth' – something that seems completely obvious to us, that it seems that nobody could reasonably disagree with – then we get upset. Despite the evidence around us every day that people from different cultures and sub-cultures see different truths about any given situation, we still want to believe that our culture's got it right, and everyone else is wrong.

In post-structuralist textual analysis, we don't make claims about whether texts are 'accurate', 'truthful' or 'show reality'. We don't simply dismiss them as 'inaccurate' or 'biased'. These claims are moral ones more than anything, attempting to close down other forms of representation without engaging with them. Rather, the methodology I'm describing seeks to understand the ways in which these forms of representation take place, the assumptions behind them and the kinds of sense-making about the world that they reveal. Different texts can present the same event in different ways, and all of them can be as truthful and accurate as each other. If all we say of them is 'accurate' or 'inaccurate', then we never get to the interesting part of the analysis – how these texts tell their stories, how they represent the world, and how they make sense of it.

The following headlines all introduced stories in online newspapers about the death of a British girl from 'CJD' – the human form of BSE (popularly called 'mad cow disease'):

'CJD kills girl, 14' (*Guardian Unlimited*, 29 October 2000)

'Millions watched Zoe's final hours' (*Electronic Telegraph*, 29 October 2000)

'BSE safety controls dropped' (*Independent* online, 29 October 2000)

To state the obvious, these are different headlines for stories covering the same event. But none of them is 'inaccurate' or 'false'. The first foregrounds the disease and the girl's age; the second personalizes her with a name, and comments on her status as national spectacle; the third puts her into a context of government policy on disease control. These are different perspectives and different representations. We can say that all three are 'accurate' but how far does that get us in the analysis, when they are obviously working in very different ways?

If there's no single correct way of making sense of any part of reality, does that mean that anything goes? That anybody can make any claim and they're all just as acceptable?

Absolutely not. This is a common attack made on post-structuralist thinking about culture, but it misses the point. Obviously some texts have very little connection to our normal ways of thinking about the world; for example, if a headline for the above story was: 'Zoe was killed by aliens: invasion imminent', very few people would think that it was accurate. There isn't a *single*, 'true' account of any event, but there are limits on what seems reasonable in a given culture at a given time. Ways of making sense of the world aren't completely arbitrary; they don't change from moment to moment. They're not infinite, and they're not completely individual. Indeed, we've got a word for people whose sense-making practices are unique to themselves and bear no relation to the reasonable ways of representing and interpreting the world in their home culture: we call them mad and we lock them up for it. That's not a cheap joke: the historian Michel Foucault's book *Madness and Civilisation* shows that people have historically been declared mad, and locked up out of harm's way when their ways of making sense of the world were radically different from those of the culture around them (Foucault, 1967). But as cultures change, so do their understandings of what are reasonable ways to interpret the world. People who are called mad in one culture – because their ways of making sense of the world are so out of step with their fellows – can become geniuses for other cultures for their convincing insights into the way the world is organized. Or one culture's mad people can be perfectly normal, everyday people in another context. In late nineteenth-century Britain: 'records of lunatic asylums show that patients included unmarried mothers' (Powys, 2002); and Edith Lancaster 'in 1895 was incarcerated in a lunatic asylum by her parents when she announced that she wanted to live in a free union [ie, not married] with a socialist railway clerk' (Bartley, 2001). Someone who would flout the social convention that women should always be married before they indulge in sexual intercourse would no longer automatically be regarded as mad, or locked up for it. Indeed, in twenty-first-century Australia, Britain or America, it would seem barbaric to lock someone up because they thought sex before marriage was OK. The idea of single motherhood is now reasonable enough that for someone to propose it as an acceptable lifestyle isn't regarded as madness. Similarly, until 1973, homosexuality was listed as a psychiatric illness – a form of madness – by the American Psychiatric Association (APA, 2002). Anybody who believed that it was possible that two men or two women could have a happy, fulfilling, loving life together was necessarily mad. Everyone knew that this wasn't the case. A strong consensus of sense-making insisted that gay relationships were sick – that is, literally unhealthy – unnatural and unworkable. Once again, in the twenty-first century, when sitcoms based on gay characters show the leads of *Will and Grace* not only as friends, but as both equally deserving of a happy relationship with a man, practices of sense-making have changed so much that you wouldn't be denounced as mad if you suggested that homosexual relationships can be as happy, stable and fulfilling as heterosexual ones.

Not everyone would agree with this point, of course; debates are always ongoing about sense-making, with differing perspectives competing to be seen as the most reasonable, and some people still think that gay men and lesbians are sick and immoral. A variety of perspective exist, but there is a finite number of sense-making posi- tions available within a given culture at a different time. So post- structuralist textual analysis doesn't insist that anything goes, that any representation is as acceptable as any other, or that any inter- pretation makes as much sense as any other. In fact, the opposite seems to me to be more the case – the reason we analyse is texts is to find out what *were* and what *are* the reasonable sense-making prac- tices of cultures: rather than just repeating our own interpretation and calling it reality.

But surely there must be some elements of reality that all cultures can agree on?

> Sometimes $1 + 1 = 0$
> Lawrence M. Krauss, Professor of Physics, Case Reserve Western University
>
> (Krauss, 1998: 149)

This is another common claim by writers who favour a realist mode of thinking about sense-making. They insist that there must be some elements of experience that everybody makes sense of in the same way. Two favourite examples are suffering and death. Because, after all, you can't stop death just by making sense of it differently; and you can't avoid pain just by pretending it isn't there.

It's odd that these arguments are repeated so often, as they are not really terribly convincing when you look into them. For how people *make sense* of pain and suffering, or of death, are vitally important to their experience of them. In fact, the cases of death and suffering present are some of the strongest arguments for the variety and importance of sense-making practices.

So, challengers say: you can't just interpret violence differently to make it alright. I'll punch you in the face and you can just interpret that away. Nobody, after all, is going to disagree that torture is undesirable. Nobody's going to suggest that torture might be nice, are they?

Are they? 'How many of us have not wondered, while watching an old war film or reading about the heroines of the French resistance, how well we would have stood up under torture, whether we would have at all?' (Schramm-Evans, 1995: 137). Thus begins the introduction to 'Sado-masochism' in the 'How To' handbook, *Making Out: The Book of Lesbian Sex and Sexuality*. Because violence – or more importantly, our experience of violence – is in fact modulated by how we interpret it, how we make sense of it:

> How we experience pain is affected by sexual arousal – the kind of pain experienced during an SM scene bears little relation to what a visit to the dentist might provide. During sexual excitement our tolerance of pain increases enormously and at the point of orgasm it may barely be felt at all. Even women not interested or experienced in SM may well have enjoyed being bitten during sex, or having their nipples squeezed harder than usual. These sensations would be highly unpleasant and unacceptable outside the sex scene, but within it they add a charge of excitement. (ibid.: 137)

Violence and pain may be pleasurable, in the right situation, in the right cultural context. Indeed, this guide suggests, it's not just that we might interpret the pain differently, but that in different contexts, it might not even exist at all. Sometimes, pain isn't pain at all – it's pleasure.

Suffering more broadly – not just violence – isn't always bad. For some harsh, but not unusual, philosophies of life, suffering is useful; or even desirable. That which does not kill us makes us stronger. 'The Bible suggests that suffering may be understood as divine discipline or instruction' (Waters, 1996: 28), and St Paul was made to suffer by God 'so that [he] learned to depend upon God's grace rather than his own strength' (ibid.: 30); for, after all, 'suffering plays an important role in one's piety' (ibid.: 31). We have to learn from our mistakes, and have the right to make them. And so on. In these sense-making practices, pain may be desirable for its reassurance that God cares.

What about death, though?

Death can't be denied simply by interpretation. It's an experience that you can't escape just by interpreting it differently. Nobody could disagree when somebody is dead for example. They either are, or they aren't. Surely.

Again, sadly, the world is not that simple. The examples I gave above showed that value judgements about pain depend on sense-making practices – whether pain is desirable or not, whether pain is pleasurable or not. The same argument can be made about death. Different sense-making cultures disagree over whether death is a desirable, or an undesirable, experience. Death of the body doesn't necessarily mean death of the person. It need not be something to be feared. It may, quite reasonably, be seen as desirable.

Of course, when it comes to those who have died, we have no idea what their experiences are. They may be identical – that is, nothing at all, lack of existence. Or they may be quite different – some in heaven, sitting with God, some in Hell, sinning with Satan. But we know that for those who are dying and for the people who are left behind, death can mean very different things. Take the case of Christianity. Knowing both that God controls every aspect of life, and that there is an afterlife with Him, it's not surprising that for many Christians death is a very positive experience: indeed, it can be a 'healing':

> A friend of mine was mortally ill and was given six months to live. His
> wife was encouraged . . . to pray with her husband daily and to lay her
> hands upon him for healing. He died almost exactly six months [later]
> . . . [and] his wife asked what healing he had received . . . She
> concluded that his quiet acceptance of the destiny of imminent death
> . . . [was] the healing he had received. (Polkinghorne, quoted in Waters,
> 1996: 50)

It can also be a 'blessing' from God (ibid.: 57): 'Our death . . . is
something we welcome . . . There is a sacred timing that should be
honoured in the ending of our lives' (ibid.: 58). This is one way of
making sense of death. For other sense-making communities, death is
deeply undesirable and must be avoided (with an extreme case being
those who freeze their bodies cryogenically, for revival when science
has progressed).

And again, like pain, it's not just a question of different value
judgements because different ways of making sense of the world in
fact disagree about when someone is actually dead; or where the line
is between things that are alive and things that are not.

Take scientists. For the non-scientists among us it might seem
obvious that some things are alive (people, animals, plants) and that
other things aren't (stones, cars, pieces of paper). These definitions
work very well as generalizations in our everyday lives to the point
that we get arrogant and start to believe that things really are that
simple, and this is a description of reality that everybody must agree
with. But scientists, who deal with the uncertain edges where things
aren't so clear, make sense of the world differently.

Professor Anne Simon – Head of the Department of Biochemistry
at the University of Massachusetts – knows that the everyday consensus about life and death is not the simple 'truth', but a rough
generalization that works fine so long as you don't think about it too
hard. She knows this because her own research is into viruses –
specifically, 'turnip crinkle viruses', with which she is very much in
love – and they don't fit into such black and white categories.
Viruses, she says: 'are simply a set of genes on the prowl':

> students often ask me if viruses are alive. I like to answer this question
> with the question 'How do you define life?' Occasionally this prompts
> the follow-up, 'Why do you always answer a question with a question?'.
> To this, my standard response is, 'Do I?'. Since this generally leads to
> vacant stares, I usually issue the reassuring statement that entire books
> have been written trying to explain the scientific meaning of life.
> (Simon, 1999: 86)

It shouldn't surprise us, then, that death is like any other part of the world – sense-making practices about death have changed over time, and differ between cultures:

> Determining when death occurs has changed over time . . . Throughout the nineteenth century and much of the twentieth, death was defined in terms of the heart and lungs . . . A person was not declared dead until the physician verified . . . that the heart and lungs were no longer functioning. Yet over the past few decades advances in medicine created an unusual and unprecedented situation. With the aid of drugs, various invasive techniques, electrical shocks to the heart and a respirator, the heart and lungs could keep going after a person's brain was 'dead'. This raised a unique question. Could an individual without a functioning brain, but whose heart and lungs continued to work with the aid of machines, be considered alive? Or even a person? (Waters, 1996: 8)

The same situation in different centuries would mean that you were dead in one, but just waiting to be revived (still alive, or still potentially alive) in another. And the debates between different sense-making practices go on: 'Under current conditions, a person is not pronounced dead until the entire brain has ceased to function . . . There are proposals to define death as the cessation of higher or cognitive brain activity' (ibid.: 9).

There is no part of reality that we can point to and say, 'Everyone can agree on this. All cultures will make the same interpretation of this part of the world. Nobody could disagree that this is how things are.' For every area of experience has multiple sense-making practices associated with it: even those that might initially seem as incontrovertible as suffering and death.

OK, no single text is simply the accurate representation of reality: but surely some texts must be better than others?

Better for what? Although it's a common everyday formulation to say that 'this is a good film'; or 'that was a bad programme'; 'this is his best novel'; or 'that is a great painting', these kind of judgements aren't relevant for the kind of post-structuralist textual analysis I'm describing here. For this methodology, you have to know what question you're asking before you can answer it (see Chapter 3). It's true that aesthetic judgements of value ('this is good/great/masterful/ his best film') are one kind of textual analysis, and one that is still taught in many Literature Departments and Film Departments. But this is a realist approach – this is *really* the best text, that is an objective claim, you cannot disagree with that – and it doesn't fit in with the methodology described in this book.

I would say that there are two main uses of these aesthetic kinds of judgement, and they tend to overlap strongly. First, we use terms like 'good', 'great', 'masterpiece' as synonyms for 'I liked that', 'I really liked that', and 'I really, really liked that', respectively. As journalist Dominique Jackson puts it: '*Talking Movies* host Tom Brookes is an informed and open-minded but demanding critic. He offers crisp, unbiased and intellectual analysis. In other words, he agrees with me' (2002: 22).

Second, there is a tradition of aesthetic judgement for analysing works of art and literature, where a set of established criteria are used to judge a text, including 'coherence', 'intensity of effect', 'complexity' and 'originality' (Bordwell and Thompson, 1993: 53–4). These criteria supposedly produce 'objective' (ibid.: 53) interpretations of texts rather than just individual response but they are still only one possible interpretation of them. This is the sense-making practice of an educated culture, one that has decided that qualities like complexity are a good thing in a text (whereas other cultures might think that 'simplicity' is more important). Ultimately, this way of interpreting texts still comes back to personal preferences (i.e. they are no more objective than simply saying 'I like this').

This tradition of aesthetic judgement can be very useful as 'cultural capital'. It can be useful to know which films have been regarded as 'masterpieces' by cultural critics, because that kind of knowledge has its own value. As the film magazine *Empire* puts it, in its monthly section, 'The Bare Necessities': 'Never seen a Fellini film? Can't be bothered trying to understand the random mumblings of Marlon Brando? No problem! Just read our cut-out-and-keep guides to bullshitting your way through any awkward social events with the black-turtleneck latte brigade' (*Empire*, 2001: 11).

It's good for your social mobility to have 'cultural capital' – to know the history of which films, books, paintings and television programmes are regarded as the best (see Bourdieu, 1984). In order to be in the trendy crowd, for example, you must have certain kinds of knowledge (about films regarded as masterpiece) and if you don't have that knowledge, circulating in a particular class of people will be 'awkward'. And so the *Empire* series tells us, for example, what is the 'reputation' of great films? ('regarded by many as a landmark in American filmmaking' (*Empire*, 2002a: 13)); 'Why is it so good?'

('what really makes it stand out is the glorious use of colour and attention to detail' (*Empire*, 2002b: 11)); 'What to say at dinner parties' ('Argento takes you to the darkest corner of your mind, the places you don't even admit to yourself' (*Empire*, 2001: 11)), and 'What not to say' ('The ballet scene is fantastic!' (ibid.: 11)). Knowledge of the tradition of aesthetic judgements can be useful but as *Empire* shows, you don't have to take it seriously to make use of it.

All in all, aesthetic judgements of texts – which are 'good', which are 'bad', which are 'masterpieces' and which are 'failures' – can be very useful for a number of cultural purposes, but they shouldn't be taken at face value as objective claims about worth, and they're not part of a post-structuralist form of textual analysis.

If there's no single correct way to make sense of the world, isn't this book just one possible approach?

Ah. Yes – you've caught me out. This book is self-consistent, and it tries to explain one methodology in detail. But it's not the only way to think about the production of meaning, or about how texts function. As I noted above, realist modes of textual analysis remain important in media studies, cultural studies and mass communication studies. For example, some 'political economy' approaches to texts insist that legislation, industries and economics are the material 'reality' of culture. Other realist forms of textual analysis see the process of interpretation as much more straightforward than post-structuralist textual analysis – assuming that the interpretation that the researcher makes will basically be the same as the interpretation that other people make. Structuralist approaches, which see deep structures across the sense-making practices of various cultures, are still also an important element of much work in our disciplines. Marxist approaches, for example, see the relation to the means of production in cultures as a basic, material reality (that is, who gets to take the profits from people's work, by dint of owning the machinery or networks that allow things to be made and distributed). Psychoanalysis sees the formation of the psyche – how our minds work – in early childhood as a basic reality that must be taken account of in writing about culture.

There is a history to this kind of textual analysis (see Turner, 1997 and Hartley 2002). It comes from a certain tradition, and can only answer certain questions. It can never do that with absolute certainty, nor can it always produce statistics to back up its claims (see

Chapter 5). There are certainly other ways to deal with texts but post-structuralist textual analysis is, I think, one useful way to answer questions about meaning-making.

Case study

John Hartley (1999) 'Housing television: a fridge, a film and social democracy', in John Hartley, *Uses of Television*. London and New York: Routledge, pp. 92–111.

Each chapter of this book finishes with a case study: an example of how to do this kind of textual analysis.

In 'Housing television', John Hartley wants to find out how texts come to be seen as 'realistic': what should a text look like in order for Western audiences to think it is showing them what reality is like? He researches this question by looking at historical evidence – a 1935 short film called *Housing Problems* – and showing that what one decade thinks is a 'realistic' text can look very dated and artificial for later decades. He makes this point by comparing how that short film represents ordinary people, compared with how they were represented in earlier texts. He performs textual analysis on this film to show that it doesn't just *reflect* reality: it finds new ways to *represent* reality that now seem obvious, but at the time were new and unusual. The film isn't just 'the truth' – no text ever is – but it's made in a certain way that makes it seem more realistic and truthful.

Hartley argues that this film represents a turning point in the processes of sense-making for British culture, released as it was in 1935, just as British television was starting to evolve into its present domestic and broadcast form. He points out that television's producers had to decide how they were going to make programmes for this new medium, and they picked up ideas from the culture around them. In fact, lots of the strategies that television uses for representing reality – including the things that it shows, and the ways that it shows them – can be traced back to films like *Housing Problems*.

Hartley points out that *Housing Problems* shows a mixture of 'public spectacle' linked with 'domestic life' (ibid.: 92). He argues that this film – as television programming would later do – represents 'ordinary' people from a dual perspective. Partly, it's concerned with large-scale issues about society (How can we live together? How can we deal with social problems?), and at the same time, it's interested in the most everyday level of lived life (so the debates about large-scale public problems aren't conducted on a completely abstract level of political philosophy).

The film . . . comprises two main sequences. The first sets up the 'problems' of the title, showing slum housing in London's East End, with a commentary by a local councillor and a succession of working class tenants speaking for themselves, telling the viewer about the lack of light, water, clean air and cooking facilities, and illustrating with vivid unscripted anecdotes the dilapidation, vermin and noxiousness, the want of privacy, sound-proofing and amenity, of their tiny flats and rooms. The second section produces what are clearly meant to be seen as ideal solutions to these problems, introduced by an unseen and unidentified 'expert' voiceover, with a professional, male, authoritativeness. (ibid.: 92)

Textual analysis is about making educated guesses about how audiences interpret texts. For example, how does Hartley know that the unidentifed voiceover is likely to be interpreted by viewers as an 'expert'? He makes this guess because he knows how this genre works (see Chapter 5). Western film viewers know that the voiceover in documentaries has a status like that of a newsreader: both are supposed to be almost the 'voice of god'. They are not really human, giving a single, fallible subjective viewpoint: we are meant to think that they are objective, simply telling us the 'truth' about the situation.

Why does Hartley make a point about the fact that the voiceover is male? Again, we know from contemporary documents (particularly around the appointment of presenters on radio) that men at this time in Britain were thought to be more authoritative, more rational, and more intellectual than women – a series of linked ideas which some people still believe.

Hartley points out that, historically, the ways in which *Housing Problems* represented ordinary people and social issues – its process of 'semiosis' (meaning-making) – were startling and radical at the time. Particularly important, says Hartley, are the film's 'immediacy' ('unrehearsed and unscripted' working-class voices); and its 'visuality': it is 'remarkably revealing', and puts on screen domestic working-class spaces that have not – literally – been seen as being fit to be shown before. There was no *Coronation Street* or *Roseanne* at the time this film was made and these sights were new ones.

In trying to understand how the language of 'reality' in this documentary works, Hartley notes that:

> Its most radical innovations are the very aspects that are now most easily overlooked, for the simple reason that what was surprising and never-before-tried in 1935 has since . . . become the bedrock of standard practice. *Housing Problems* uses real people, not actors. They are named in the film, which lets them speak in their own words, in their own houses, not to a verbally tied-up, editorially vetted and visually shaped script. It treats a mundane object seriously, ordinary life with respect, and working class people without patronization. (ibid.: 94)

Again, we can only make educated guesses about this text. It may be that some viewers of the film will think that it *is* patronizing to the working-class people shown: Hartley can only claim, as he does, that based on his understanding of the codes of representation, of the ways in which a media-literate audience of the time was expected to understand certain codes, that it is not *likely* to have been seen that way. Drawing on contextual evidence, he points out that:

> In 1935, ordinary people did not participate in public culture without a script. Every interviewee on BBC radio, for example, had to follow a script, even if they were engaged in what was intended to sound like an impromptu or improvised conversation. Ordinary people, speaking for themselves, were almost unknown in mainstream cinema . . . The idea of putting real people on the screen, without the mediating 'help' of a seen interviewer, to articulate in their own words the truth of their circumstances, was indeed an innovation. (ibid.: 97)

As he points out, the textual features that he is describing are an almost perfect fit with what we now call an 'actuality segment' or 'reality TV' (see *Airport*, *Sylvania Waters*, *The Village*, etc.). But this representation of 'reality' is not simply 'real' – it is a set of practices and techniques for making texts, with its own history – which begins to emerge in the UK with this 1935 documentary film.

Hartley also notices how the meaning of elements of texts can change. Discussing the history of British housing, where crowded inner city slums were cleared and the tenants moved into new, badly serviced and designed 'housing estates' and 'tower blocks' that had, in many cases, much worse social and health problems than the slums that they replaced, Hartley notes that:

> With severe conviction and militant self-confidence [the film] wants to clear away slum conditions. But the shots it uses to demonstrate how uncomfortable and intolerable such life is for tenement dwellers – shots of women sweeping and beating the dust out of rugs in the back alleys, while the children play and muck around – these are the very scenes which the next generation claim as illustrations of the solidarity, community and supportive mutuality of working class life. (ibid.: 95)

Hartley draws on historical texts – accounts of social life – in order to contextualize and help make sense of the text he is analysing. He notes that:

> the slum clearances which began in the early 1930s, and which were continued after the war into the 1950s and 1960s, struck at the physical heart of 'family' and 'neighbourhood'. It was only later that commentators started blaming 'the media' – television especially – for the dislocated culture, 'broken' families and hostile neighbourhoods of some working class life. (ibid.: 95)

By drawing on contextual evidence – other relevant texts – from the time of this film's release, Hartley is able to show that it holds an important place in changing representations of the people of Britain. It develops a visual and editing vocabulary that was taken over into television, and now represents an important part of our everyday sense-making of the cultures in which we live: through television news, current affairs, documentaries and ever increasing numbers of 'reality TV' programmes. None of the representational strategies of these programmes – letting non-experts speak, doing so informally, showing working-class living spaces in the public sphere – are simply, obviously, 'realistic'. They have a history of developing that claim. By looking at one of the texts that contributed to that history, and making an educated guess at likely interpretations of it, Hartley uses a post-structuralist form of textual analysis to provide evidence for his research on this kind of representation.

Each chapter of this book ends with three sections. The first, 'And the main points again', is a summary of the arguments presented in the chapter. The second, 'Questions and exercises' gives you some work to do to develop and expand on the points made, and allow for a bit of active learning. The third, 'Textual analysis project' leads you through a complete work of textual analysis in the course of the book, in simple, step-by-step stages in each chapter.

And the main points again

1   All cultures and subcultures have different ways of making sense of the world: from the most extremely different (Indigenous Australian and British, for example), to the most subtly different (men and women, for example).
2   We can respond to this fact either by insisting that our own 'sense-making practices' are the only correct ones (a 'realist' or 'cultural chauvinist' approach); by looking for the common deep structures that underlie these different systems of sense-making (a 'structuralist' approach); or by accepting that other cultures do experience reality differently (a 'post-structuralist' or 'cultural relativist' approach).
3   If we are interested in how cultures and subcultures make sense of reality differently, we can gather evidence for this by analysing texts.
4   Texts are things that we make meaning from, from books to television programmes, to items of clothing, to buildings.
5   No text is the *only* accurate, true, unbiased, realistic representation of any part of the world; there are always alternative representations that are equally accurate, true, unbiased and realistic.

Questions and exercises

1   Spend an afternoon listening to the radio. Tune in not only to
    your usual station, but to the stations aimed at different groups:
    talkback radio stations, easy listening music, news channels,
    youth music stations. Spend some time listening to each one.
    Make a detailed list of the differences in their assumptions about
    the world. What do they think is interesting to listen to or talk
    about? What issues do they raise? What views do callers present?
    Are callers allowed to talk at all? What is challenged by the host
    and what is left unchallenged? What kinds of language do they
    use? Make a list of things you hear that just seem so ridiculous
    that surely nobody could believe them.

2   Go to a newsagent. Browse through the magazines, and see what
    subcultures they serve. Buy a few (or, if you're lucky, find a library
    that stocks them). Get one that speaks to a group that you don't
    belong to, and that you wouldn't normally read. If you're male,
    buy a woman's mag; if you're female, buy a man's. Get one that's
    aimed at an interest group that you have never heard of (if I had
    never picked up a copy of *Modern Ferret* magazine, I would never
    have realized that a community of ferret-fanciers existed, what an
    important part ferrets played in their lives, nor how much of their
    social, ethical and even political thinking was tied to their ferret-
    owning pursuits). Again, make a detailed list: what do these cul-
    tures think are worth reading about? What assumptions do they
    make about their readers? Does this group have an enemy that
    they have to struggle against? What does the magazine say is
    different between its readers and other people? What function
    does the magazine serve for the community? How do readers see
    the magazine? (Look at the letters pages.) Does the magazine
    engage with party politics, the government, issues of policy? Or
    does it focus on private and personal life?

3   Go to a library. Find more than one newspaper from the same
    day (it's best if they serve different contituencies, for example,
    get some local and some national papers; or tabloids and broad-
    sheets; or left-wing and right-wing papers). Find their coverage of
    the same story. Write a detailed list of the differences between
    the stories: what elements do they emphasize in their headlines?
    What photos do they use? Whose voices are heard? How many
    different perspectives are given? With whom is the reader meant
    to sympathize? And any other elements that seem relevant to

you. Choose the story that seems to you to be most 'unbiased'. Does it fit in with your own beliefs? Or do you disagree with its position?

4 Do the same thing with newspapers from more than one country – how do they cover the same story differently?

5 Go on the Internet and go to www.google.com. Type in the phrase: 'the truth of the situation is' (including the quotation marks), and press the 'Google search' button. Visit a number of the websites that contain this phrase. How often do writers use this phrase to present a truth that doesn't fit in with how they personally see the world? How often do they use it as a synonym for 'This is how I see the situation'?

Textual analysis project

1 Write down some topics about culture and how people make sense of the world that interest you.

Which parts of culture, and which questions about it, interest you? This can come from academic reading, or from your own experience of culture. Textual analysis can provide information about the way in which culture works; the way that particular groups or parts of the world are being represented; or about how people are making sense of the world ('sense-making') more generally.

Familiar questions that academics use textual analysis to answer include those that concern party politics (How are particular political parties represented in the media?; How is an election campaign covered?; Which forms of social organization are presented as most attractive in the media?) and identity groups (How are men/women/lesbians/older people/etc. represented in the media?). But if you have interests in other areas, the beauty of textual analysis is that it can be applied to any texts to answer any question about sense-making (analyse different versions of the Bible to see how ideas about the relationship between God and man have changed over hundreds of years; analyse graffiti in toilets to see how cultural differences between men and women work in these private spaces, etc.). Read lots of histories and theories of culture for new ideas, perspectives and questions.

2   Focus your question to become more specific.

Let's say your initial question was 'How does the media contribute to men's sense of what it means to be a man?'. That would be a massive research project. Try to make it more focused, both by limiting the number of texts you are discussing, and looking for a specific question that you can actually find an answer to.

Avoid vast questions that want to generalize about the whole of culture. Even before we start studying and researching culture, we all have a lot of knowledge about how the media works in our culture – promoting stereotypes, avoiding positive images, dumbing down and looking for the lowest common demoni-nator . . . please forgive me if I exaggerate for effect – forget it all. This attitude is based on profound ignorance.

Think honestly – what do you actually know about how people consume texts? You've probably got a series of prejudices in your head – the masses are hypnotised by television, magazines and tabloid newspapers that sensationalize and trivialize stories because readers are stupid and have short attention spans . . . again, please allow me to exaggerate to make a point, and insist that all of this is rubbish. Everyone thinks that other people are affected by, and mindlessly consume, the media in this way. Nobody actually does it. If you want to find out how readers actually make sense of texts, then you need evidence about that (see Chapter 4). We think that we can just say, 'our culture represents men like this'. But you really can't generalize very easily about these things, and it will take years of research before you know enough about the vastly different kinds of masculinity in culture across, for example, news programmes, soap operas, women's magazines, men's magazines, self-help books, DIY manuals, Rotary club newsletters, etc., to make these kinds of generalizations. When you're starting out, it's best to keep focused, and try to answer specific questions, that you can find specific answers for. For example: 'How do "lad mags" teach their readers to be men?'

Note

1 Those three descriptions were the hardest part of this book to write. These questions have been discussed for over a century in a number of university disciplines, and even writers in the same disciplines don't always use the same words to mean the same things. On top of all this, the words are borrowed and used with different meanings across disciplines. Because of all this, it's impossible to produce labels for these tendencies that will make sense to all readers in all disciplines. The descriptions I've chosen are fair enough uses of the words within cultural studies, literary studies and anthropology – and, I hope, everyday language. They don't fit in well with the way these words are used in philosophy: better labels for philosophers would be (in the same order): cultural chauvinism; anthropological structuralism; and cultural relativism (Gibson, 2002)

Does it really matter how people make sense of the world? 2

Why does it matter how people make sense of the world?

In our Western cultures, we think that how people make sense of the world is very important. In fact, this post-structuralist axiom (assumption) is now becoming a kind of common sense for us. We believe that how you make sense of your experiences is important for whether you're happy with your life, and the way that you make sense of other people is an important element in your behaviour towards them.

How we interpret our life experiences is important for our own survival
This belief is so much a part of common sense that we even have a word for it: 'self-esteem'. The phrase itself isn't new: 'Self-esteem', meaning 'favourable appreciation . . . of oneself' (*Oxford English Dictionary*) has been in the English language since at least the seventeenth century. But now it's taken on a distinct usage for mental health professionals as an important part of understanding people's behaviour. Textbooks emphasize how important it is that children must be educated to develop their own self-esteem – they must be taught that they are appreciated and valued for the kind of people they are. They must learn to interpret their own experiences and qualities as being valuable and worthwhile in the culture in which they live. This must be done because – the health sciences insist – otherwise they are at greatly increased risk of 'suicidal ideation' and behaviour. If people are constantly told that they're worthless – either personally, or because of the group in which they live – then they may accept that information, and make a decision not to carry on living.

Between 20 and 35% of gay youth have made suicide attempts, the best available statistics show . . . Youthful gays often internalise negative stereotypes and images of themselves. And when you have been told that you are 'sick, bad, wrong for being who are you are', you begin to believe it. (Herdt, 1989: 31)

For mental health professionals, it's now generally accepted that: 'low self-esteem [that is, how people make meaning of their own life, value, existence] is associated with depression and may contribute to suicidal behaviour' (Crocket and Petersen in Brown, 1996: 14). This is almost a post-structuralist approach to health – these health professionals insist not only that how people make meaning of their experiences is vitally important, but also that the job of healthcare workers is not to force them to fit into a single dominant kind of sense-making. For example, these health professionals don't insist that homosexuals are bad, so all young people must get married and pretend they don't have these feelings. Instead, they encourage everyone to value their own ways of making sense of the world.

Of course, this post-structuralist approach is not the only one that can be applied to thinking about mental health. We could also insist that people shouldn't think about things so much; that they should favour actions over introspection and just get over it, get up, go to work, get married, have children. Don't think about whether or not it fits in with your own view of the world. But the promotion of self-esteem – focusing on the importance of meaning-making practices – continues to grow. Self help texts, from books to television programmes such as *Oprah*, continue to place sense-making at the centre of our lives. *Oprah* also favours another, similar term – one that's played an important part in many of the social justice movements that have emerged in Western cultures in the course of the twentieth century – 'role models'. The idea that the representations we see of groups to which we belong can provide us with models for our own behaviour is now common sense.

Similarly, politicians and economists are starting to move towards a post-structuralist approach to the importance of meaning-making. For, as we know, money can't buy you happiness: and a recurrent worry in journalistic representations of our society is that these two things don't seem to be directly linked: 'the 1990s has been a decade of economic growth, real wage gains and asset price rises – yet the community has often seemed to be more unhappy amid such material progress' (Kelly, 2002: 6). Initiatives like the Genuine Progress Indicator (GPI) have attempted to challenge a traditional kind of economics that measures the well-being of a society purely in terms of its material possessions:

> [The GPI] attempts to capture the impact of economic activity on the quality of life . . . the GPI deducts [from economic figures] the negative value of events that detract from wellbeing . . . [for example] crime subtracts from wellbeing by heightening insecurity . . . the GPI was an attempt to answer the question. If things are going so well, why doesn't it feel like it? (Morris, 2000: 5)

An ongoing concern with 'happiness' is a part of Western cultures: for, as a woman's magazine's front cover story on the pay-rise for *Friends* stars puts it, they are: 'So rich, yet so miserable. New $90,000 per minute deal is proof money can't buy happiness' ('Miserable millionaires', 2002). The number of self-help books that aim to increase your self-esteem, and help you to gain 'happiness', is massive (my favourite title is *You Can Be Happy No Matter What* [Carlson, 1997] – it's a spooky promise that makes me think about going to your child's funeral with a huge smile on your face). The shift from money to happiness in social policy insists that it's not what you *have* that matters – but how you *make sense of* what you have: how you think about it, and how you feel about it. This is very post-structuralist – and, again, it's not an extreme or 'mad' form of sense-making. It's already at the centre of Western cultures' (and particularly American culture's) sense-making practices. How we interpret things is important, we know, for the value of our own lives.

We also have common-sense phrases about how important our sense-making practices are. Kath Albury, for example, discussing the ways that we learn gender roles in culture, suggests that: 'We can't opt out of the system that insists on labelling us . . . gender and sexuality are culturally policed, and if you step out of line, someone will let you know about it – even if it's a little nagging voice in your own head' (2002: 114). A 'little nagging voice' isn't a scientific phrase, but it is a common-sense one, and to understand it, we have to understand that how we think about things matters, and has very real, experienced effects.

At its most extreme, making sense of the world differently can even change it physically. At the ceremony of Thaipusam in Singapore, Hindus have their bodies (cheeks, etc.) pierced with spikes and needles: 'metal hooks or spikes are fastened onto the skin, or through it. Devotees may also pierce the tongue and/or cheeks with a small silver vel . . . shaped like a spear . . . At this festival, they go into a trance, ordinarily feel no pain, and oddly enough rarely bleed or scar' (Craig, 1979: 126, 128). Again, sense-making practices are not irrelevant to the reality of how the world is. They are an important part of our survival in the world.

How we make sense of other people is important to how we then treat them

To take a very practical, and very extreme example: what should you do if you're taken hostage? How should you behave in order to maximize your chances of surviving such a situation?

According to the Queensland Police Department in Australia, one important point is that you should – as the situation allows, and without annoying them – tell your captors your name, and a bit about your life. If they see you as a human being, with a name and a life – rather than as an object in their larger plan – they will be less likely to harm you physically. The way that they see you – whether that's as person or as an object – can have vital implications for your chances of survival. Sense-making, again, is not the opposite of reality: it is the very condition for living in it.

From the opposite side, police training to deal with 'cults' insists that it's vitally important how the police view these groups. Writing in *The FBI Law Enforcement Bulletin*, three FBI training agents describe how important sense-making is to avoiding bloodshed in police practice. A 'cult', they say:

> may be defined as a movement that is foreign to the culture in which it lives . . . Many groups that Americans once thought of as 'cults' – such as the early Quakers, Seventh Day Adventists or Mormons – have received increased recognition and acceptance and become accredited churches. Other groups, such as Zen Buddhists, which many Americans may view as 'cults' represent mainstream movements in other parts of the world. (Szubin et al., 2000: 1)

This is a post-structuralist perspective, being placed at the heart of law enforcement. These 'cults' are different cultures, favouring different sense-making practices, which are defined precisely by their difference from dominant sense-making practices in their host culture. But, of course, they might be central forms of culture in other nations – and might become more central in our own cultures (as the Mormons have done).

From this post-structuralist perspective, the ways in which police officers think about, and even how they name, these groups of people, can have very real, very material effects. For there is: 'a common tendency to view "cults" with a combination of mistrust and fear . . . such misconceptions . . . may be dangerous when harboured by law enforcement officers charged with dealing with these groups' (ibid.: 1). Trainers are now trying to persuade police to stop thinking about 'cults', and think of them instead as 'New Religious Movements' (NRM). These two terms aren't just synonyms. There are implications of danger and irrationality in the word 'cult': 'the word "cult" . . . carries with it a set of negative connotations: "cult" leaders are con artists; "cult" followers are brainwashed sheep; "cult" beliefs are bizarre or ludicrous; and "cult" movements are dangerous, tending toward suicide or violence' (ibid.: 2).

By contrast, the term 'New Religious Movement' is a more tolerant and open description. The police trainers think that it really matters which of these sense-making practices is employed by police officers for to think of 'cults' can actually have (to use these FBI officers' own word) 'dangerous' effects: including death in several case studies that they go on to describe. Because the officers expected conflict, they got it. By contrast, in another case study, the police in the town of Garland, Texas, viewed the Chen Tao movement(/cult) that moved into the town as *citizens* with rights to be protected rather than as a weird cult. They met with, and spoke with representatives of this group, and when God failed to arrive in His flying saucer on the 31 March 1998 (as they expected He would), the event passed without incident. Again, sense-making is central to living in reality.

The importance of how we make sense of elements of the world, and how this can affect the way that we treat other human beings, could be illustrated with thousands of examples. A couple more come from one of the less obvious categories of texts that I mentioned in the first chapter of this book – clothing. Clothes are not simply material objects – they are also texts. We interpret them, and make sense of the wearer – perhaps reading messages that they want us to read (if someone dresses to try and be sexy, and we find that they are); or messages that they don't (if someone dresses to try and be sexy, and we interpret their efforts as pathetic and unconvincing). A T-shirt with words on, for example, 'Don't look at my breasts' – is obviously a text: it demands interpretation, and we make meaning from it. But a T-shirt *without* writing on it – perhaps a very short, very tight white T-shirt, worn with Levis 501s – may be a text that can be interpreted to make a guess about somebody's sexuality. A suit might be a text – whether it is appropriate or inappropriate, trendy or conservative, expensive or cheap; as might a pair of shoes: if a man turns up for work wearing stiletto heels, it is very likely that this will be noticed, commented upon, and an explanation sought for it.

How we interpret somebody's clothes can have important implications for how we then treat them:

> Luisa Passerini's study, *Fascism in Popular Memory* . . . [discusses] the memory of an Italian woman worker of the clothes she wore to work, and the ideological situation of that apparently mundane aspect of daily life . . . The factory at which she worked had refused to provide overalls and she had worn a red pair of her own. She recounted how: 'They had called me into the office: they asked me why I was dressed in red. In fact, I'd always gone into the office in my red overalls and they didn't like it. So that time in the studio, they asked me: "And is it because you are a Communist?". I replied, "It's because I like red".' (Middleton and Edwards, 1990: 20)

How somebody makes sense of the colour of your clothing can lead to your sacking, or worse.

How about this: could the fate of the free world depend on what clothes one person decides to wear, and how other people interpret them? That how people interpret what somebody wears could be so important that it could influence the future of world politics?

It might seem like a ludicrous scenario: if political reporters in 2002 didn't suggest that it was actually the case. Following the US war on the Taliban in Afghanistan after terrorist attacks on the World Trade Center on the 11 September 2001, Afghanistan was left without a leader. It was necessary, for any attempt at continuing peace in the country, to find somebody who could appeal to various distinct groups in the country. The interim leader who was appointed, Hamid Karzai, became a focus of great media attention: and part of this attention was about his clothing. How to interpret what this man wore? One political reporter suggested the importance of his clothes:

> Karzai's wardrobe was carefully co-ordinated for a set of serious purposes. His tribe, the aristocratic Popolzai clan of the Pashtuns, hails from Kandahar in Afghanistan's south. The flat-peaked karakul pelt hat and shimmering purple and emerald capes, called chapans, he sports are typically worn by Tajik and Uzbek tribesmen, who come from the north. The tunic and loose trousers he favours are a nod to the rural people of his country. The double-breasted blazers he often pairs with them demonstrate his strong Western influence. Such sartorial gestures of inclusion are typical of Karzai, who is keenly aware of the importance of his statement dressing. (Sally Jackson, 2002: 12)

This leader has to appeal to diverse constituencies, to look as though he can represent all of them. The way in which these people think about him, from seeing his image, becomes tremendously important (most of them won't know him personally, and so can't judge him in that way). This text – his outfit – has a vital political role to play. How people make sense of this is neither an abstract nor a trivial issue: it could mean the difference between the success or the failure of the interim regime in this war-torn country; and this could have massive ramifications for the stability of a number of political regimes in Muslim countries, and thus for their relationships with the USA.

How we make sense of ourselves in relation to others is important for living in a human society
An important meeting point for these two concerns – how we think about ourselves, and how we treat others – comes in the increasingly important concept of 'identity': what groups we belong to, and who else we allow into those groups with us. We fit ourselves and other people into labels that we develop in our cultures – for example, black and white, men and women, gay and straight – and then think about ourselves, and about them, differently because of that.

But those labels are biological, surely? They don't just change with culture – they're a natural part of reality, aren't they?

No. They're not universal across cultures. Like everything else, there are many different ways that we can group people, and we can see this by looking at other cultures.

For example, race is a cultural construction, not a biological one. A white person can travel to another culture, and find out that they've become black:

> History tells us about . . . South Africans born into one racial classi-fication only to be reclassified as a different race later on in their lives by the apartheid government; about the politically expedient designation of Japanese people as 'honorary whites' by the apartheid government . . . about someone who changes races when she crosses national boundaries (Mexicans are considered people of color in the US, but were classified as white in apartheid South Africa; an Argentinean might be white in her home country, but 'Hispanic' in the US). (Barnard, 1999: 205)

The same thing is true for gender. In everyday Western culture, there are two sexes: male and female. We often take a realist perspective:

this is just reality (or 'biology' or 'nature' or some similar word). But other cultures have different categories for sexes. In some parts of India, for example, there are three sexes – male, female and 'hijra' (Nanda, 1993). In Western countries, one baby in every two thousand is born neither male nor female – they are hermaphrodite, asexual or intersexed – and we operate on them to make them fit into our cultural categories. And again, scientists – who have to work with the messy details of the world, rather than our easy everyday general-izations – tell us that our familiar labels don't simply reflect reality. When you consider the many elements that make up 'sex' – chro-mosomes, primary sexual characteristics (genitals), secondary sexual characteristics (fat, muscle and hair distribution) – and the amount of overlap that can occur between all of these categories, scientists suggest that we really should have more than two labels. Biologist Anne Fausto Sterling, for example, suggests that we need five sexes if we're going to follow biology in our labelling of people (Fausto-Sterling, 2001).

Labels about sexuality also change over time and across cultures. Homosexuals didn't exist until the nineteenth century. There was sex between men and sex between women before that time – but that didn't make them gay. Historians tell us that in Classical Athens, if a man had sex with a younger, socially inferior boy, it was considered to be what we would now call a heterosexual act (although it didn't have that label at the time) – it was normal, expected, socially approved of. That man would also be expected to have a wife, and to have sex with her. But if he had sex with an older man, or a social superior, that was perverse (Halperin, 1989). The word 'homosexual' was invented in 1892 (the word was first used by Krafft-Ebing, in his *Psychopathia Sexualis*), and the idea that this was a particular kind of person, who would only want to have sex with people of their own sex, evolved.

Like other texts, the labels that we apply to people (including ourselves) in order to put them into groups are different in different cultures. None of them just reflects reality. And – as with people who find that their race changes in different counties – we can learn to fit into new identity groups if need be. It doesn't happen overnight: but it does happen. We interpret texts in the culture around us to find out what groups exist; and then we make sense of our lives in relation to them:

> In 1924, F O Matthieson . . . described the impact of reading Havelock Ellis' *Sexual Inversion* . . . 'Then for the first time it was completely

brought home to me that I was what I was by nature [i.e. gay] . . . How clearly I can now see every act and friendship of my boyhood interpreted from my proper sexual temperament'.

Reading a text meant that this author had to go back and 'interpret' his life experiences again, allowing him to make sense of his experiences in a way that reassured him that there were other people like him in the world.

Why are identities important?

Like 'self-esteem' identity can be important for mental health. If we don't see representations of people that we think are 'like us'; if we're not offered an identity that we can claim, and a group that we can belong to, then we can end up mentally unhealthy: as in the case of the Peace Corps Volunteer mentioned in Chapter 1:

> Trying to see things the Filipino way soon becomes a real threat to one's identity . . . The typical [Peace Corps] Volunteer cherished directness, sincerity, efficiency, and quality. Yet all these values were challenged by the foreign culture in which he [sic] worked, to the point where they could be counter-productive. Realising this, the volunteer was likely to pose for himself some searching questions, such as 'If all I do is play a part, adjusting my behaviour to my hosts, then what will I be contributing to the community?' And 'Should I be, and can I be, a good enough actor to be false to what I value as right and good?'. And ultimately . . . 'Can I not be myself?' – which inexorably led to the unnerving: 'Who am I?' (David Szanton, quoted in Roces and Roces, 1985: 86)

The recognition of a group 'identity' to which you can belong is currently seen to be a vital part of mental health. Feelings of 'isolation', 'anomie' and a lack of 'social integration' are important risk factors for young people at risk of suicidal behaviour (Huffine, 1991: 42, 46). How we make sense of our identity isn't an abstract issue: it has real effects.

Identities are not universal – they are elements of culture. And new identities proliferate: for example, since gay men and lesbians fought for civil rights, it's now possible to identify as (and to be understood, if you identify as) gay, lesbian, bisexual, queer, transvestite, transsexual, transgender, omnisexual or celibate. Identities like 'grey power', an increasing number of differentiated categories for differently abled people (both physically and mentally), and distinctions within existing identities (you may be a man, but are you a lad or a SNAG?) have contributed to an exponential increase in available identites. Some of the most important that are currently available in Western culture relate to:

- gender (almost everyone knows if they are male, female or refusing the categories);
- race and ethnicity;
- class (particularly in Britain, but to a lesser extent the existence of 'white trash' discourses in both Australia and America means this form of identity isn't entirely absent there either);
- age (it often seems as though youth and elderly people are at war, at least in news coverage);
- nationality;
- sexuality;
- physical ability.

As well as allowing us to feel that we belong, we also use identity categories to guide us in our treatment of other people. As John Hartley puts it, Western cultures are involved in an ongoing process of creating 'wedom' and 'theydom' (1992: 206): describing the people who are like us, and excluding the people who are not like us. And we tend to interpret the behaviour of 'us' very differently from how we interpret the behaviour of 'them', even if they do exactly the same things. We're much more forgiving and empathetic towards people that we think are in our own community, and far less tolerant, and more punitive, towards people that we think are 'them'. The most obvious example of this is when countries go to war. For example, at the time of writing (July 2002), America is engaged in a 'war against terrorism'. It's estimated that, to this date, many more Afghani civilians have been killed than the 3216 Americans who died in the initial terrorist attack that began the hostilities (the plane crashes into the World Trade Center on the 11 September 2001). And yet the media coverage of those civilian casualties has been nowhere near that covering the deaths of the initial casualties – in terms of extent or emotional investment. Of course, there are many complex reasons for this – questions of intent, general ethics of behaviour in different cultures, and so on. But there's also an important underlying factor: in a war, the behaviour of 'our' people is justified, brave and heroic, even if it causes regrettable 'collateral damage' (civilian deaths); but the behaviour of 'them' – terrorists or soldiers from another country – is unacceptable.

A similar thing happens every time we watch a news programme: what happens to 'us' (people in our own country) is always more important than what happens to 'them' (people in other countries). One death in our country may well make a headline; a single death in another country probably won't (unless it's an important political or media figure whose death has some implications for 'us').

But such examples might be too extreme, too far from the every-day. We make such judgements all the time in our everyday lives as well:

> [Australian swimmer] Ian Thorpe smashes a world record and Australia hails him as the next world hero. Dutchwoman Inge de Brujin follows suit and Australian swimming is sceptical. Australians are always quick to condemn athletes suspected of drug-taking, but slow out of the blocks when it comes to our own. (the *Australian*, 11 April 2001: 5)

Sense-making isn't an abstract part of our lives, and it isn't a luxury afforded only to a few. It's part of existing as a human being. How we make sense of our own lives, and of other people's, has vital impli-cations for our own well-being and for how we treat others. At its most extreme, we can see the importance of the construction of communities of 'we' and 'they' when a sense-making practice sets up a binary between 'we' as human beings and 'they' as non-human: 'In a recent court case in Cameroon, the judge ruled against a woman being allowed to inherit property, saying, "Women are property. How can property own property?"' (Abdela, 2001: 20). The judge is quite correct within his own sense-making system – how can a piece of property be said to own things? The fact that most of the readers of this book will find such a sense-making practice both alien to their own practices, and extremely offensive, makes clear just how important the ways we make sense of the world can be.

If sense-making is important, how do texts relate to that? Do media texts have an impact on people's thinking? Or are they expressions of the way they already think?

Much study in the disciplines of mass communications and media studies – as well as some cultural studies – works on the assumption that the texts that surround us have an important effect on the way that we think. Often this is given as a kind of simple physical equa-tion – *this* message is broadcast and then people begin to think in *this* way. There's an assumption that if only the media changed the kinds of stories that they told, then people would start to think differently. This is the propaganda model of the media.

This isn't really convincing – there's no evidence that such a straightforward causal relationship exists between the texts that people interpret, and their sense-making practices. I prefer to use the metaphor of language to think about how it works.

There are limits on the reasonable ways that we learn to think about particular elements of our culture. So, for example, the death of Zoe from CJD, mentioned in the previous chapter, can be understood as an unfortunate accident; or as a result of government policy failures; or as the personal responsibility of her family, who did not adequately protect her from this danger; or as a blessing or healing for her (from a Christian perspective), and so on. But other ways of thinking about that death – that purple aliens are responsible, that doctors deliberately killed her as part of an experiment – are far less likely to seem reasonable. Then again, there are other ways of thinking about this death that would be reasonable in other cultures – in Indigenous Australian cultures, for example – that would make very little sense to a Western person who had not encountered those. The culture that we learn – just like the language that we learn – places limits on the sense-making practices that we indulge in:

> Japanese women speak a different form of the Japanese language from that spoken by men . . . women spea[k] to men using different gram- matical structures involving . . . extra polite vocabulary to an extent designating almost feudal subservience. This begs the question of whether a Japanese female manager could ever succeed in giving a direct order to a male, and presents a long-term and deeply rooted difficulty for Japanese women seeking workplace equality. (Irwin, 1996: 79)

So using this metaphor of language, if somebody broadcast a tele- vision programme, or published a book, which was in a completely new language (or relied on completely alien forms of sense-making), then it would be literally meaningless. Nobody would be able to understand it. Just as we all speak the language we learn, but express our own thoughts and ideas through it, so we learn what are reas- onable sense-making practices in our culture, and think within them. And just as language is always evolving, so sense-making practices keep changing. But nobody can simply decide that they will begin speaking a new language tomorrow, and expect that it will catch on. New words enter the language, but not in a systematic way. No one person controls how many new words will enter the language or where they will come from (although institutions like schools, and dictionary editors, attempt to do so, with varying degrees of success). In the same way new ideas, and different approaches to sense-making, enter the culture – but not in a systematic way, and not under any one person's, or one group's, control: 'All of us . . . operate within cultural constraints, just as we all share conventions of speech . . . [someone] may push a language to its limits, but at some point he [sic] will hit against the outer frame of meaning. Beyond it, madness lies' (Darnton, 1985: 14).

Using this metaphor, then, I don't think that media texts control how people think. The media texts, like the sense-making practices of individuals, have to work within the practices that already exist, although they can also try to alter those. The process is like a feed-back loop: texts in the media have to draw on existing ways of making sense of the world: these are then interpreted by people, and feed back into the texts that they themselves produce (speech, writing, dress codes); and then these feed back into mediated texts . . .

Nicholas Reeves' book, *The Power of Film Propaganda: Myth or Reality?* (1999), is useful for thinking about this question. His study looks at film-making in Britain during the First World War; in the Soviet Union in the 1920s; in Nazi Germany; and in Britain in the Second World War. These propaganda films were produced with the specific intent of changing how people thought about particular elements of the world – making the enemy seem more demonic and the troops seem more heroic. They were active attempts to intervene in sense-making practice by producing texts with a deliberate message.

Reeves tries to work out how successful these attempts were, by examining audience reports, opinion polls and discussions about these films. He concludes that:

> successful film propaganda proved remarkably elusive. Where it set itself the modest task of reinforcing existing ideas it did, on occasion, enjoy greater success. Even here, however, audiences constructed their own meanings in the films that they saw and thus it was the audiences, not the propagandist, who determined whether or not propaganda would succeed. (Reeves, cover)

From a historical perspective we can see that some texts have had a particularly important effect on the way that groups of people made sense about the world, and even how they behaved in that world. We have to bear in mind, though, that trying to trace causes and effects in human thinking, behaviour and culture isn't like a chemistry experiment. We can't carefully introduce texts as an experiment to one culture, while keeping another identical 'control' culture unchanged. We can't keep every other element of a culture static and unchanging while we do the experiment. So claims about possible causes and effects of cultural change can only ever be educated guesswork. From studying the history of various kinds of political movements in Western countries, for example, and considering them in relation to television texts, John Hartley suggests that:

> Coming out of the 1950s . . . television showed the domestic audience something of 'nature', as it was innocently called in those far-off days . . . long before Jacques Cousteau. Now we have environmentalism, eco-warriors and the million-member RSPB (Royal Society for the Protection of Birds) – 'nature' with political teeth, backed up by quite unusual public tolerance for activism, by groups such as Greenpeace, 'Swampy' and others, and unprecedented dialogue between governments, corporations and activists in the formulation of public policy, for instance around the fate of the Shell vessel *Brent Spar*, and roadbuilding policy in the wake of the by-pass era. Of course, David Attenborough didn't 'cause' all this, but it is my belief that year after year of Anglia's *Survival*, Oxford Scientific Films, the Nature Unit productions at Bristol, not to mention the strange 'nature-logues' imported from all continents of the earth to the hearths of East Finchley . . . have 'ameliorated [improved] our manners', in this case, persuading millions of the need to tread more lightly on the natural environment, and to temper production with conservation. (1999: 180)

Another example of the way in which particular texts might have changed sense-making practices is the television programme *Star Trek*. Interviews with scientists at Massachusetts Institute of Technology (MIT) suggest that many of the people currently working in science became scientists because of their love for this programme, and its utopian image of technology's role in social progress (Cuthbertson, 1999: 3; Jenkins, 1995: 213). Indeed, Constance Penley goes so far as to argue that the whole attitude towards space exploration in America, and indeed the very continued existence of NASA, are only possible due to the optimistic, technologically progressive vision of the future and of space travel that has been presented in the various *Star Trek* programmes over the past forty years. She traces a number of ways in which explicit links between NASA and *Star Trek* can be found:

> people who work for NASA are perhaps as Trekked-out as people anywhere, perhaps in part because *Trek* lore and language lends itself

well to a work culture devoted to the science and technology of space exploration. Mission Control computers have been called Scotty and Uhura, and the shuttle's on-board computer is named – what else? – Spock. The working name of the proposed sequel to the Hubble Space Telescope is 'Space Telescope Next Generation'. And many of the astronauts have been vocal about the inspiration they received from *Star Trek*. Mae Jemison, the first African-American woman in space, says that it was Nichelle Nichols in her role as Lt Uhura, the African communications officer on board the Enterprise, who first made her want to go into space [. . . She also] began every shift of her shuttle mission with Lt Uhura's famous line 'Hailing frequences open' . . . the first shuttle [was named] Enterprise. Many of the show's cast members were there as the Enterprise . . . was rolled out onto the tarmac . . . to the stirring sound of Alexander Courage's theme from *Star Trek*. (Penley, 1997: 19)

Penley argues that *Star Trek* provided a way of thinking about something that didn't exist at the time of its conception – manned space flight – which was attractive and exciting. This provided Americans with a framework that they could use to make sense of attempts to get into space. Indeed, she goes so far as to suggest that: '*Star Trek* is the theory, NASA the practice' (ibid.: 19).

Again, as with Hartley's argument, this can't be 'proved' in a scientific way: but as I note above, nothing to do with human beings and their meaning-making processes really can: certainly not in large groups like those that form 'cultures'. This shouldn't be lamented – scientific procedures are only one form of knowledge production, after all. But it must be acknowledged.

So I would argue that occasionally, a text or a group of texts can be shown to have been particularly important in changing sense-making practices in a culture. But we must also remember that it works the other way around as well: audiences, with their continual, everyday sense-making practices, have a huge effect on the production of texts as well. Media producers deliberately try to produce texts that will fit in with the sense-making practices of audiences – they don't just produce whatever they would like to see, or push particular ideological lines that they believe.

And most texts don't have these large-scale effects on sense-making practices. Not every text is equally important in a culture. Most of the texts that surround us engage in the everyday, background ongoing feedback loop of the maintenance and slow evolution of ideas and sense-making. You can't use texts to programme how people think, or how they behave. It's impossible to predict which texts will be particularly important, or to predict exactly what effects they will have. Once again, we can offer educated guesses: but we must always be open to being surprised by the workings of culture.

In short: I think that by analysing a text you can find out about the sense-making practices that were in place in a culture where it is circulated as meaningful. But from analysing a single text, I don't think you can make confident statements about any effect of that text on the way that the people who consumed it thought about themselves or their lives. Texts that draw on similar kinds of representation can be used in very different ways. To discuss those kinds of questions, you need to look for the evidence of other related texts (like the interviews with NASA *Star Trek* fans mentioned above).

But industries like advertising, marketing and public relations make millions of dollars by claiming that they can have effects on people's thoughts and behaviour – how can that be?

Exactly – they make money. They have to claim that they can predict with certainty how their texts will affect people. That's the product they're selling: certainty. And they're selling it to the companies who employ them – not to consumers. In *Buy This Book! Studies in Advertising* (great title), Mica Nava quotes William Lever from household goods producers Lever Brothers (one of the biggest advertisers in America for several decades). He says: 'Half the money I spend on advertising is wasted. The trouble is, I don't know which half' (Nava, 1997: 39). In fact, this uncertainty is something that Nava insists is central to advertising as an industry: because there is: 'remarkably little correlation between sales and the amount of money spent on advertising' (ibid.: 40): 'The picture of the advertising industry which emerges with remarkable consistency from its own accounts, its trade magazines, interviews with workers at all levels . . . is one of extensive demoralisation, fragmentation and suspension of disbelief' (ibid.: 40).

Advertisers don't know exactly how a particular text will function when it is set loose into the public sphere with any more scientific accuracy than I do. They don't know if a television advertisement will – like the classic 1980s Levi 501's campaign that had Nick Kamen stripping in a launderette – treble sales and become a massive hit in its own right, or if it will bomb and have no effect. Like textual analysts, advertisers draw on their knowledge of the market to make educated guesses about likely interpretations of, and responses to, texts. But it remains – as advertisers themselves insist – an art, and not a science.

Answering the question about why companies would continue to spend so much on advertising when its own claims to certainty are not backed up by evidence, Nava points out that from her own research with advertisers: 'Advertising is as much about promoting the corporate image of a company to its rivals, clients and employees as it is about selling commodities to the consumer' (ibid.: 40).

It's the same with television programmes. The producers of television texts – even the most successful of these people – can never say with any certainty what will be popular. Aaron Spelling is the Executive Producer of *Melrose Place*, *Dynasty*, *The Love Boat*, *Charlie's Angels*, *The Mod Squad*, *Beverley Hills 90210* and many more. He's in the *Guinness Book of Records* as the person who has produced more hours of television than anyone else in the history of the world. Attempting to explain the success of one of his own programmes – *Melrose Place* – he has this insight to offer: 'What drives all this *Melrose* mania? Phenomena such as this are always a bit of a mystery – otherwise all TV shows would be hits. My own *guess* is there's something else going on besides all the sexy stars and surprising subplots' (Spelling, in Wild, 1995b: viii, emphasis added). It's only a 'guess' that Spelling can offer – although, of course, it's an educated guess. Similarly, despite the extremely long, complicated and profits-driven process by which a programme like *The X-Files* makes it on to television (the complexity of the rules, the equations, the training of all the business people involved in trying to work out scheduling, demographics, market share and so on) Sandy Grushow, the president of Fox Entertainment Group, says: 'You're always surprised when one of these things [TV programmes] hits the way *The X-Files* has hit . . . It's hard to know for sure. Anybody who says they do is lying or a fool' (in Lowry, 1995: 19–20).

Particular texts can help change sense-making practices in a culture. But such change will always be relatively slow. You can't completely revolutionize sense-making practices in a culture using only a small number of texts: and certainly not when the choice to consume particular texts is voluntary. And there's always some element of unpredictability in the interpretive practices of a culture. Human beings are sense-making creatures, and although we can make educated guesses about uses and interpretations of particular texts, these can never be confidently predicted with mathematical equations.

We know that processes of interpretation are complicated: academics have been studying it for decades. Shakespeare, for example, may have an 'effect' on someone, but it depends on how they read his work, how they have been trained to read literary texts, what else they have read ('this reminds one of Milton's comments about Satan' – but only if 'one' has read Milton), how they think the different texts are linked to each other (borrowing, appropriation, pastiche, plagiarism, reinvention, etc.), and so on. There are many factors to take into account. The same is true when we study interpretation of mass culture texts, although we sometimes forget this. It would seem odd to ask 'What effect does Shakespeare have on his audiences?', but we still sometimes ask 'What effect do violent movies have on their audiences?', as though there was no process of interpretation involved in making sense of something like *The Matrix*. Obviously there is.

I would insist that every process of interpretation is complex and unpredictable, although at any given time it will also be within predictable *limits*. People interpreting Shakespeare do so by drawing on relevant knowledge, their readings of other Shakespeare plays, their knowledge about drama generally, wider culture codes. And people interpreting *The Simpsons*, do the same thing – by drawing on relevant knowledge, their interpretations of other television comedy programmes, their knowledge about drama generally, and wider cultural codes. Interpretation is a complex business.

Are all sense making practices equally good? Is a sexist world-view just as good as a feminist world-view, for example?

This is a difficult question. Most of the disciplines which use textual analysis for their research have some kind of political commitment. Mass communication studies desire an orderly society where deviance (for example, violence) can be properly managed. Media studies writers often desire a properly democratic society, where the media serves traditional forms of politics in the most transparent way. Cultural studies researchers are often the most overtly political of the researchers who use textual analysis, pushing for more equitable forms of social organization. Some of these writers demonstrate a Marxist concern for working-class citizens; others for a variety of identity politics that want to see social justice for women, black citizens, gay men and lesbians.

It is perfectly true that from a post-structuralist perspective it's not possible to make unreflexive truth statements about what constitutes a better form of society. You can't just say: 'It's simply the truth that women are equal to men', and leave it at that. As I explained in

Chapter 1, a post-structuralist perspective means that different ways of thinking about the world might be equally valid. So what do you do when you think that particular ways of making sense of the world are unethical, or unacceptable, for example, societies which deny women the right to an education? Or cultures which execute gay men?

In practice, researchers who employ post-structural methods of research feel just as passionately about political issues as those who employ realist or structuralist modes of analysis. The major difference, it seems to me, is in the kinds of argument that you can use to try and convince people of your case. Put simply, you can't try to persuade people that they should change their behaviour simply because they are *wrong* and you are *right*. You have to find other ways to persuade them to think differently.

For example, say I am unhappy with the way in which many Australians think about the Indigenous people of Australia – thinking that they are inferior people, that they are drunks, that they don't deserve the money ('my taxes!') that they get from the government, and so on. In my own sense-making practices, I think that Indigenous culture managed to be self-sustaining and stable for forty thousand years before European invasion, which suggests to me that the fact that many aspects of Indigenous culture in Australia are currently so problematic – such as the fact that the life expectancy for an Indigenous man is twenty years less than that of a white man in Australia – must be due to the history of invasion and conquest in Australia. Fine. What am I going to do about it?

From a post-structuralist perspective, I have to accept that my own sense-making practices are not simply, 'the truth'; rather, it's the position that currently seems to make most sense to me, based on my information about the area. I have to accept that the people who make sense of this differently from me are not just stupid, or ill-informed, or evil – they may have their own informed and ethical reasons for making sense of Indigenous Australian culture differently. So although I know that certain aspects of my own thinking may change over time, or may be challenged by finding out new information, if I feel strongly that the sense-making practices of other people are dangerous for Indigenous Australians, it's my responsibility to try to persuade them to change their thinking. This is the key issue. From a post-structuralist perspective, you're not in a position to tell other people that they're simply wrong. You've got a much harder job: to try to find arguments and information that might persuade them to come round to your way of thinking. It must be a process of attempting to win consent, rather than trying to force people to think differently, using a big stick of 'truth' and 'facts' that they don't know. And, at the same time, you have to be open to the possibility that you might *learn* something from the people that you're talking to: that in the conversation where you try to persuade them, they might actually end up persuading *you* to see things a bit differently. Without this possibility of mutual exchange, I don't really see much possibility of changing other people's sense-making practices.

All of which seems to me to make perfect sense, because ultimately, the only way you can change someone's thinking is by persuasion. You can't use physical force to make somebody think differently (psychologists are beginning to say that the very idea of brainwashing is a myth, and it isn't possible to change somebody's thinking in the long term by physical methods like sleep deprivation – see Bromley and Richardson, 1980). And from looking at public debates, for example, in the letters pages of newspapers, it's obvious that when people are convinced that they know the truth on a particular matter, they rarely convince anybody else to change their mind. Letters claiming that somebody is missing the 'truth' of the situation, or the 'reality' of it, which is in fact that . . ., usually lead to letters responding that, No, it's the letter writer who's missing the truth of the situation, which is in fact that . . . And opposing positions are stated, and restated, and stated again, with no compromise between them.

Many writers in cultural studies have attempted to intervene in the sense-making practices of populations. Some writers have wanted to change the kinds of texts that are published, particularly by journalists in newspapers and in television news, wishing for texts which are less racist, less sexist, less homophobic, less capitalist, for example. Although it's possible to imagine that such a change in the production of texts could be an important intervention in sense-making practices (so long as they were made in such a way that people wanted to watch them), in practice, such calls rarely lead to much change. I guess that this is because the work of so many of these academics is very adversarial. Working from the assumption that texts make people think in particular ways (see above), many cultural studies researchers have decided that it must be the journalists who are responsible for the kinds of sense-making that happen in a culture and therefore, journalists are racist, sexist and homophobic, writing racist, sexist and homophobic stories (even though the majority of journalists, just like the members of most other creative professions, are left-wing). This must stop!, these researchers insist. And, of course, journalists don't take any notice, because they've just been insulted. The researchers are setting up an adversarial relationship, taking the moral high ground against the journalists, and telling them what to do – and all of this without any understanding of how texts are produced in capitalist culture so that audiences might choose to consume them. It's no wonder that in a number of Media Forums organized by John Hartley and myself in Australia – which aimed to bring together journalists and Indigenous Australians to try to improve relationships and representations of both sides – journalists were always very suspicious of the academics who attended. They knew that these academics were the enemy, because the academics themselves made it so very clear.

Cultural studies researchers have also been involved in other forms of intervention in sense-making. Producing your own texts – online, in community media, as fanzines or letters to the editor, or artworks – adds to the number of different sense-making practices to which people might be exposed. The work of John Hartley has provided an interesting model for pragmatic political work on culture. Hartley has been involved in a number of initiatives to attempt to intervene in sense-making practice, from working on radical newspapers to film-making, always paying attention to the specifics of particular situations, asking how the sense-making practices he's concerned about might actually be changed. So, for example, in a research project on the representation of Indigenous Australians, Hartley's attempts to change sense-making practices weren't confined to sitting on the sidelines shouting insults at journalists for being 'racist'. Instead he organized workshops where journalists and Indigenous people could meet; published non-academic resource books full of practical information from interviews with Indigenous media producers that journalists could use; initiated the gathering of information for a list of contacts of Indigenous journalists, that mainstream media outlets could draw on to get a wider range of Indigenous comment; and organized a high-level national meeting of Indigenous political leaders, that allowed the media to see Indigenous culture as one with a national political leadership.

Another important way in which it is possible to intervene in practices of sense-making, and one in which cultural studies in particular has been very active, is through teaching or what used to be called (by women's groups and gay and lesbian groups in the 1970s) 'consciousness raising'. Many of the cultural studies researchers who are now recognized as founding figures – such as Richard Hoggart and

Raymond Williams – worked in adult education colleges in the UK, teaching working-class men and middle-class women about culture, what it meant, and how to use it. Rather than changing the texts that were produced, they attempted to change how people interpreted them. This desire to intervene in practices of sense-making by means of teaching has remained strong in cultural studies (see Hartley, 1999). It's what we often do in our classes. It's what I'm trying to do with this book. But as I say, from a post-structuralist position, I can't do that simply by asserting that 'This is the truth, you are wrong'.

My own position, as someone committed to post-structuralist thinking, but with strong political beliefs of my own that I will happily try to explain to anybody who will listen, is a very liberal-humanist Amnesty International kind of stance:

> Amnesty International is a worldwide campaigning movement that works to promote all the human rights enshrined in the Universal Declaration of Human Rights and other international standards. In particular, Amnesty International campaigns to free all prisoners of conscience; ensure fair and prompt trials for political prisoners; abolish the death penalty, torture and other cruel treatment of prisoners; end political killings and 'disappearances'; and oppose human rights abuses by opposition groups. (Amnesty, 2002)

I believe that tolerance is desirable, as is finding ways to build consensus and live together in our larger communities. Unwanted suffering should be limited. The good of the many very rarely outweighs the good of the few. All people's cultures should be approached as equal. The desire to hurt other people, physically and emotionally, is undesirable (unless they want to be hurt). Ultimately, everyone has the right to decide what is good for them. The ideal world is one in which a desirable state of life – whatever state of life each person's culture consensually accepts is desirable – is experienced by as many of its members as possible. That ideal world will never exist. Simple answers are fine for most general situations, but we always have to remember that they are not 'the truth', and there will be situations that will have to be weighed up on a case-by-case basis.

The only desires that I cannot countenance are those which demand that, in order to make one person happy, another person should not be allowed to exist. And I am quite happy to support social and cultural experiments, as long as they are conducted in an ethical manner (so, no putting people up against the wall and shooting them just to see if that would make the world a better place).

In short, my position might be described as a post-structuralist humanist culturally-committed democratic liberalism. (I should point out here for Australian readers that being liberal is not the same thing as supporting the Liberal party. I mean that I like the concepts of democracy and freedom and, I hope, I'm 'free from unreasonable prejudice in favour of traditional opinions or established institutions; open to the reception of new ideas or proposals of reform', as the Oxford English Dictionary puts it. These are not qualities favoured by Australia's Liberal party.) Within these abstractions, I think that there's no single correct answer for any given situation, but that a pragmatic approach should aim for results, rather than imposing standardized morality without caring whether it works or not.

I believe strongly in all of these points: but I cannot, in all good faith, insist that they are simply the 'truth' of the world. I can present arguments and evidence defending them, and I'm interested in understanding at what points other people might disagree with me, and why? I know that my own politics have changed remarkably over the past decade, and I must remain open to the possibility that they may do so again. These positions are always necessarily provisional: but that doesn't make them any less real, any less strongly held, or any less important to me and my sense of who I am.

Case study

Jane Shattuc, 'Sobbing sisters: the evolution of talk shows', in her *The Talking Cure: TV Talk Shows and Women.* (1997) New York and London: Routledge, pp. 13–46.

Jane Shattuc's history of talk shows attempts to suggest why programmes like *Oprah* and *Ricki* are so important for women in Western democracies. These kinds of representation, she says, are more accessible to women than traditional forms of political discussion (serious, sombre, unemotional, abstract and disengaged); and this is precisely why they matter so much. Because they open up public discussion to an audience that has previously been excluded from it, they're an important part of democratic culture. She makes this argument by drawing on analysis of 240 hours of American daytime talk show texts, including *Oprah*, *Donahue* and *Geraldo*.

Shattuc's argument relies on the fact that different subcultures within a nation can have quite different sense-making practices. Her example here is gender. Shattuc draws on contextual information from political philosophy to show that politics has traditionally been a 'masculine' part of culture. We know that certain kinds of argument and knowledge are often thought to be 'masculine' – rational, abstract, public, factual debate – while other forms of argument and knowledge are traditionally feminine – emotional, personalized, experiential, caring, empathic and personal ways of thinking and talking. This is not to say that all women are emotional and all men are rational. But it's common sense to associate emotions with women, and rationality with men: 'Given that men are reluctant to discuss their emotions, they are left with two major topics of conversation – the weather and sport', as *Cosmopolitan* magazine puts it (July 1997, p. 134).

Shattuc's textual analysis shows that the forms of debate favoured in talk shows are traditionally feminine ones. Issues are introduced through personal examples – single individuals – rather than as abstract ideas:

> the structure of an *Oprah* program is typical of most daytime talk shows: problem solution. Most often, the problem is introduced as a personal problem (for example, HIV+, a bisexual spouse), but then generalized to a larger social issue . . . For instance, an April 15 1994 program on mothers who want to give up their violent children becomes generalized by Oprah to 'What really makes a child act this way?' Either by taking the opposite side or teasing out other views, Winfrey questions the guests to flesh out the problem. (ibid.: 95)

Traditional forms of expertise – detached and rational positions, guaranteed by positions of authority, either political or academic – are not recognized in these programmes as the most important ways of justifying an argument. Rather, it's personal experience and personal feelings that become the most important guarantors of truth:

> Talk shows represent a change in the concept of social truths . . . the distant evidence of expert knowledge is no longer valid . . . audience members privilege individual experience as the primary source of truth . . . [this] allows Oprah's Prozac-taking audience members [in a programme on the drug] to 'disqualify' the experts for having only 'academic knowledge' of the pain of depression. When Dr Peter Breggin (author of *Toxic Psychology*) declares: 'Oprah, people want to believe – we want to believe that it is a biochemical imbalance', the Prozac-takers respond determinedly 'It is!'. So powerful is the belief in the power of personal experience . . . that the audience knows more about the chemistry of psychopharmacology by virtue of experience than does a psychiatrist who is a leading authority . . . As one *Oprah* audience member stated on April 14 1994: 'Don't tell me how I feel. I am my experience'. (ibid.: 1997: 98, 99, 100)

The programmes don't ignore larger social issues – but they approach them from the viewpoint of individuals who have personally experienced them, instead of discussing them in the abstract: 'It is only the slow process of individual audience members getting up and testifying to their similar experiences that leads to the concept of a larger community – society at large – and evidence of a social problem or issue' (ibid.: 98–9).

Oprah doesn't seek out the truth of an issue: rather, she tries to find consensus – another practice which is traditionally feminized in Western cultures:

> In general, *Oprah* offers a subtle form of 'we' achieved through her slow process of consensus building . . . The spontaneous breakthroughs increase as audience members in Wenatchee call the show and in the studio jump to the mike and emotionally acknowledge their use of Prozac. As one woman states, 'My secret is out'. The rising tide of testimony not only leads to a truth based on sheer numbers, but also to a truth based on experiences that are real, and not on the expert's numbers and sociological language . . . The Prozac program relies on a classical relay where the guests on the stage initiate the emotional displays that center on the subject: Prozac use. Then an invited Prozac user in the audience makes an angry retort to the assertion that Prozac causes a false personality. Intensity builds with more testimonials as to the normalcy of the Prozac experience until one has the sense that . . . America, and particularly its female citizenry is a nation of born-again, well-adjusted but highly emotional people on Prozac. (ibid.: 97, 99)

Having shown that these texts draw on 'feminized' forms of argument and evidence, Shattuc then points out that the forms of sense-making associated with women's culture (the emotional, the personal, the domestic and the experiential) are generally dismissed in public debate. Talk shows are dismissed within masculine culture as part of: 'the whole "degraded" landscape of schlock' in American culture (Frederic Jameson, quoted, in Shattuc, p. 14): '[c]onventional notions of evidence exclude the personal as [being] subjective and not representative. *Oprah* turns these notions around by offering spontaneous and raw evidence' (Shattuc, 1997: 98). Talk shows serve an important function, Shattuc argues, because they present public issues in ways that women have learned to be comfortable with. It actually matters, she says, that the forms of sense-making associated with women's culture are allowed a space in the public sphere and are validated there. Shattuc thinks this makes it much easier for women to access the public sphere and to take part in political debates: whereas the traditional insistence that their sense-making practices are worthless and trivial has made it more difficult for women to enter the public sphere: 'the shows . . . represent a profound political change: the authority of everyday lived experience . . . [and] the empowerment of the knowledge of people who are not formally educated' (ibid.: 109). The term 'empowerment', like 'self-esteem', emphasizes the importance of sense-making practices: not of changing your material circumstances, but of changing how you think about them. Shattuc shows how the talk shows themselves offer this to their viewers: the idea that sense-making can be important:

I think other women can help women to feel good about themselves. Other women can pitch in and help women go through the process of self-creation. (Janie Wavel, 'Psychologist for minority girls', ibid.: 111)

Women discuss and debate 'the problems of self-esteem for little girls' on *Oprah* on April 19, 1994 . . . 'I see myself in Janeesa' [an eleven-year old guest] says one speaker. 'You know, when I was younger than Janeesa I used to hate my nose. I will tell you this: you grow into it, Janeesa. I used to try to put a clothes pin on my nose to make it go up because I used to think that people who had pointed noses were better than people who do not'. (ibid.: 113)

Shattuc's textual analysis places the talk shows in the context of public debate in order to examine the ways in which they discuss issues. She draws on wider sense-making practices about gender and public affairs, and uses extensive evidence from the texts themselves, in order to show that this genre of television presents a feminized version of public debate and that this is still unusual on television. She also shows that there are many voices, within traditionally masculine forms of public debate, who dismiss or insult these programmes for their feminized form. And she goes on to suggest just how important these programmes might be, because they offer a sense-making practice within public debate that makes it easier for women to engage in that debate.

Two points to finish with. First, there's never a 'correct' answer to questions about value judgements. For Shattuc, the feminization of public debate is an important move in making the public sphere more demo-cratic, and more accessible to more people (especially women). But for some other writers, this is a bad thing. They think that feminized forms of argument really are worthless and should be kept out of the public sphere; that these shows are not serious enough; that they individualize and emotionalize public issues; and that this is all a very bad thing. They interpret it as the 'degradation' of civic life (Giroux, 2000: 136), 'person-al[izing] and . . . trivial[izing] serious debate' (Becker, 1997: 13), par-taking in 'empty talk' (Goldfarb, 1998: 210). Everyone can agree that these shows use a feminized form of communication but the question of whether this is a good thing or a bad thing can never be finally resolved.

Second, the questions that you ask to some extent determine the answers that you will find. Shattuc is only answering one question. This isn't an analysis of everything that could possibly be said about *Oprah*. Joshua Gamson, for example, analyses the public construction of sexual identities on talk shows (Gamson, 1998); Tony Wilson researches the national identity of talk shows, looking at cross-cultural reception con-texts (Wilson, 2001); and Wendy Parkins is interested in *Oprah*'s part in the construction of spirituality in modern society (Parkins, 2001). It isn't possible simply to 'analyse a talk show' or any text. We always bring particular questions to bear, and find answers for those questions. There are always different perspectives that can be taken in any textual analysis. Which takes us neatly on to the next chapter.

And the main points again

1 It matters how people make sense of the world. It matters for their own health; and it matters for the way they treat people around them.
2 One important aspect of sense-making is identity. We put ourselves and other people in groups, and treat them differently because of it.
3 These groups are not just 'natural'. They change over time and across cultures.
4 The media doesn't control sense-making practices.
5 Individuals don't control sense-making practices.
6 Like language, sense-making practices in cultures evolve slowly, and no one group is in control of that change.
7 Not all sense-making practices are equal: you have to decide for yourself which are more desirable, and attempt to persuade other people to your point of view by using arguments and information – not just telling them that you're right and they're wrong.

Questions and exercises

1 Make a list of the identities that are available in your culture (e.g. male, female, black, Asian, white, and so on). Which ones are simple binaries (either/or)? Which ones have more than two choices? Which ones are usually set for life (e.g. male/female)? Which ones can change?
2 Which do you think are the most important in your culture? Which impact on people's lives the most? Which give them most guidelines about how to behave and treat others? What identity groups are treated worst in your culture (paedophiles? refugees?)?
3 If a man goes out with a younger woman, then he is often thought to be behaving normally. If a woman goes out with a younger man, she is often thought to be looking for a toy boy. Make a list of examples of this tendency – where the same behaviour is judged differently depending on which identity group you belong to.
4 Go to the list of new words added to the online *Oxford English Dictionary* – http://dictionary.oed.com/public/help/Dict/Quarterly/0206.htm. Scroll half-way down the page to 'Out of sequence new

entries'. This gives you a list of some of the new words that have recently entered into the English language. Many of these involve new sense-making practices – making sense of the world in ways that didn't previously exist. Print this out. Then go to http:// dictionary. oed.com/entrance.dtl. Type some of these new words into the box in the top left-hand corner of the screen, and press the 'Find word' button. The dictionary will give you the earliest recorded list of this new word/idea; and other places where it has appeared. Who is making up these new words/ideas, and how are they spreading into the language?

5 Make a list of texts that have had an important impact on you and changed the way that you make sense of the world. Who produced these texts? What kinds of effects have they had on you?

Textual analysis project

1 Write down some topics about culture and how people make sense of the world that interest you.
2 Focus your question to become more specific.
3 List the texts that are relevant to your question from your own experience.

Obviously for 'How do "lad mags" teach their readers to be men?' you need to gather copies of lad mags. So you would start off by listing all the lad mags that you know of. Even at this point, you'll start to draw on your own cultural knowledges, and it's already becoming important that you have a familiarity with the area you're describing because you have to decide what counts as a lad mag. Do you want to include older men's magazines (like *Playboy*) in that category? Or do you think that they're completely separate?

4 Find more texts by doing research both academic and popular.

Find any previous academic writing on the topic – that will give you more titles of lad mags and relevant magazines. Search the library catalogue with keywords; and then do 'sideways scanning' (go to the bookshelf and look sideways at other books with the same call number). Search on the Internet. Check out any other sources you can think of (go to a newsagent's and browse). Come up with a list of as many lad mags as you can.

What's interpretation got to do with it? 3

If we're collecting evidence of how texts represent reality, can we just describe what happens in them?

The story so far: textual analysis is a methodology for gathering information about sense-making practices, that is, how members of various cultures interpret the world around them. We analyse texts using a form of 'forensic' analysis – treating them like clues (or 'traces') of how people have made sense of the world.

The problem: there's no single correct representation of any part of the world and, in the same way, there's no single correct interpretation of any text. The ways in which members of different cultures may make sense of a text will vary just as much as the ways in which they make sense of the world around them. When you're doing textual analysis, you have to remember that different groups will probably have interpreted each text in different ways.

Audience researcher David Morley showed an episode of the British current affairs television programme *Nationwide* to a number of different groups: the episode included a story about the 1977 British Budget. The groups interpreted this story in different ways. A group of union shop stewards thought that it was 'biased', because it took a right-wing approach to the topic. A group of bank managers thought that it was problematic too but only because it didn't go into enough depth on the topic. They didn't think it had any bias. A group of (mostly Black) further education students thought that the whole programme was 'boring' – it had nothing to do with their lives – but beyond that had little to say about the Budget story (Morley, 1980). These people were all interpreting the text in different ways. None of these interpretations is 'correct'. They're all reasonable i[nterpreta]tions of the same text. Doing textual analysis, we're int[erested in] finding out likely interpretations, not in deciding which [is] the most correct one.

But surely if we describe a text in the most simple, objective way possible, everyone could agree on it?

Every description of a text is an interpretation. If two researchers described the same text, they would do it in different ways. It's very unlikely that they would come up with exactly the same words in exactly the same order to describe it.

The interpretations of the *Nationwide* episode made by Morley's groups are not that different. They didn't agree if the story was interesting, or if it was objective: but they did agree that it was a story about the tax system. This is because these interpretations are produced by members of different subcultures who aren't really that far apart (they might be different ages and different classes, but they're part of the same nation, same language group and same gender). But if we compare interpretations of a text made by very different cultures, we can see that there's no description of a given text that everyone from all cultures can agree on.

Anthropologist Eric Michaels worked with a Warlpiri (Indigenous Australian) community to see how they thought about films and television programmes. He describes his reaction to a video made by local Warlpiri cameramen:

> Warlpiri videotape is at first disappointing to the European observer. It seems unbearably slow, involving long landscape pans and still takes that seem empty . . . Yet Warlpiri audiences view these tapes with great attention and emotion, often repeatedly . . . The camera in fact traces tracks and locations where ancestors, spirits or historical characters travelled. The apparently empty shot is full of life and history to the Aboriginal [viewer]. (Michaels, 1988: 120–1)

To a European-trained viewer, the shots are empty. If Michaels – or most Western viewers – had been asked to just describe, in the simplest possible terms, what was in such a text, they would have said 'nothing', or 'rocks', or 'landscape shots'. That's a definition that would work well within Western cultures – most Western watchers of such a text would agree with you. It would seem obvious and commonplace – we're just describing what we see.

But for a Warlpiri viewer, a straightforward description of the same shot would be very different. It would include elements that are simply not there for the Western viewer. Such a straightforward description would include a mention of the Dreaming track that is shown in the text, and the places where various important historical and mythical events happened. Neither of these descriptions is simply 'the correct one'. One person sees a rock, another person sees a Dreaming track. Each will produce a different, simple, straightforward, description. To an Indigenous viewer, the shots are full of life and history. If you're familiar with a series of other texts – Dreaming stories about the landscape – then the videos offer up all kinds of meaning. But if you don't know those texts, and instead interpret the Warlpiri videos through your knowledge of Western entertainment videos then they appear to be completely different texts – empty of possible meaning.

Michaels shows that the same process works in the other direction. He describes the differences between his interpretations of the Hollywood film *Rocky* and those made by Warlpiri viewers:

> Narrative [in Warlpiri stories] will provide detailed kinship relation-ships between all characters, as well as establishing a kinship domain for each. When Hollywood videos fail to say where Rocky's grand-mother is, or who's taking care of his sister-in-law, Warlpiri viewers discuss the matter and fill in the missing content. By contrast, personal motivation is unusual in Aboriginal story: characters do things because the class of which they are a member is known to behave this way. This produces interesting indigenous theories to explain behaviour in [for example] *The A-Team*. But equally interesting, it tends to ignore narra-tive exposition and character development. (ibid.: 119)

To a European viewer, in the Sylvester Stallone film *Rocky*, Rocky's grandmother doesn't exist; to an Indigenous viewer, she is offscreen and must be placed into the story. Again, the interpretations are so different that they even make the text different: the grandmother, for the Warlpiri viewers, does exist. She's a necessary part of the text; she's just offscreen.

These are extreme examples, to illustrate an important point: you can't do anything with a text until you establish its context. You can't even simply describe it without implicitly putting it into a context (for example, the Warlpiri video – if you simply described it as 'empty', or 'shots of landscape', you would automatically be putting it into a Western context). Even within nations, various different identity subcultures can also have distinct enough sense-making strategies to produce quite different definitions of a text. One example is sexualized sense-making communities – straight commu-nities and queer communities – in reviews that attempted to describe what the film *The Adventures of Priscilla, Queen of the Desert* was about. It was, on the most abstract level, a film about three people going across a desert in a bus. But how would we describe these people? For some reviewers, the film was about 'three drag queens' (Mohl, 2002): for others, it was 'two drag queens and a transsexual' (Imdb, 2002). A reviewer who describes the three characters as 'three drag queens' is obviously not part of a queer community: any self-respecting member of the queer community would know that there are important differences between a drag queen and a transsexual. From outside that community, if you don't know much about it, then such differences are less visible. Another review describes the characters as: 'three female impersonators' (Winters, 2002). Again, you couldn't be part of a queer sense-making community and describe the film like that: in the queer community, drag queens and female impersonators aren't the same thing (drag queens are more aggressively masculine in much of their performance). It's also interesting (well, I think it's interesting) that none of the reviews describe the characters as 'two men and a woman'. Even though the character of Bernice in this film is physically a woman – she's had a sex change operation – it's obvious from these reviews that this interpretation (post-operative transsexuals are, in fact, women) isn't common sense in Western cultures yet.

Every straightforward description is also, necessarily, an interpretation. We must always try to understand the variety of possible interpretations, and the most likely ones for various communities and not just repeat our own interpretation (description) of the text. In short – don't just describe elements of a text. Textual analysis is not just textual description.

But there must be a correct interpretation of each text?

In some university disciplines, the teaching of the correct interpretation of a text is central to understanding that text. You are taught what interpretations previous generations of scholars have made, and these are presented as the most convincing and most worthwhile ones.

In traditional forms of English Literature, and in much Film Studies, the most important interpretation of a text is the one that the creator of the text – the author of the book or the director of the film – makes of it. By finding out what the creator says about the text, the researcher then has a privileged insight into understanding it –

what it's *really* about, and what various elements of it *really* mean. I have fond memories of failing an undergraduate essay in English literature because I produced an interpretation of a John Keats' love poem that read it as a piss-take of romantic poetry: the metaphors were so clichéd, the ideas so obvious, that it read to me like a parody of that kind of writing. Of course, this was not what Keats intended the poem to be, and would very likely not have been a common interpretation at the time the poem was published. But I stand by the interpretation as a likely one, if the poem were widely circulated in twenty-first-century western cultures. The Professor wasn't saying that my interpretation was anachronistic; he wasn't saying that I was interpreting the poem from the wrong perspective. My interpretation was just wrong. That is not what the poem means, this is not what Keats meant, he told me as he failed me.

This 'authored' approach to texts isn't the only natural or obvious way to study them. It's only one possible approach. The idea that the creator of a work of art has a privileged insight into its meaning is a relatively recent one, historically speaking (Foucault, 1984: 101; Praz, 1951). It isn't possible to *prove* that the creator's interpretation of a text is the correct, and the most important one. And it's not possible to *disprove* it either. The question is based on value judgements that you either accept or you don't. Of course, we know that audiences do make multiple interpretations of texts. And we know that often these will disagree with the interpretation made by the creator of a text. The question is, are these variant interpretations just *wrong?*

For this form of textual analysis, they aren't wrong. If we want to understand how people are making sense of the world, then dismissing the interpretations that they make as 'wrong' doesn't help very much. Textual analysis takes the opposite approach – it wants to find out what interpretations are produced, and which ones are most likely in a given cultural context. Again, this assumption is inherent in the very word 'text'. A post-structuralist approach to meaning-making doesn't accept that any text has a single correct interpretation.

Some examples might make clear why I think that the creator's interpretation of a text isn't necessarily the most important one. Situation number one: evaluative differences can exist between the creator of a text and consumers. At the level of evaluation, it's obvious that if we just take a creator's intent as being 'the truth', then we effectively wipe out the entire cultural sector of criticism. We would just have to ask the creator 'is your new book good?', and let them say yes or no. For example, Julia Louis-Dreyfus says of her appearance in the film *Hannah and Her Sisters* (Woody Allen, 1986) 'I had this *tiiiny* little part, and I really screwed up'. Reporting this, *Seinfeld* fan David Wild adds, 'Of course she did no such thing'. But if *she* says the performance was really bad, then . . .? (Wild, 1998: 80).

Situation number two: the creator of a text produces an interpretation that doesn't agree with the interpretation produced by many of the consumers of the text. For example, *The Bill* is a long-running British police series set in London. It has had a positive effect on police relations in the UK:

> As its everyday story of policefolk continued to attract a large and loyal audience, the [London] Met[ropolitan Police] realised that the show was helping its officers and those from the other constabularies. That is not, and never has been, the producers' intention, which is to provide an entertainment, an alternative to the soaps and the glossier drama series on the airwaves. But they're not knocking it. (Kingsley, 1994: 27)

Viewers are interpreting the programme in a way that the producers didn't expect – they think it's a suitable tool for making sense of their own relations with the police, and find the representation of the police in the programme to be a positive one. This isn't what the producers intended. Does this mean that the viewers are wrong? In a way, they are – they're not making sense of this text as the producers expected, or intended that they would. Does that matter? Not for the producers: they're happy for viewers to do this. Should it matter to us? Should we continue to insist that the interpretation of the producers is the only correct one? It's a very limiting approach if we want to understand the circulation of texts in culture.

Another example is Chris Carter's work on *The X-Files*. In his episode 'Darkness falls', Carter writes about a plague of killer insects that are freed by logging work. This episode was awarded an Environmental Media Award in 1994. These awards are presented to programmes 'with an environmental message' (EMA, 2002): 'that increase public awareness of environmental problems and inspire personal action on these problems'. In order to win, a programme must 'clearly deliver an environmental message in some way'. The members of the EMA believe not only that 'Darkness falls' can be interpreted as providing an environmental message, but that it does so 'clearly', and is likely to 'increase public awareness and inspire personal action'. But these judges are wrong – at least, if we accept the producers' interpretation as the correct one. For as the creator and producer of *The X-Files*, Carter can pretty clearly be placed as its author and he explicitly states that this episode 'was not designed to push a message about conservation' (Lowry, 1995: 146). So the judges – who interpreted it as not only having that message, but having it clearly enough to possibly change people's behaviour – are wrong. Aren't they?

Situation number three: what do we do with those situations where the producer abnegates all responsibility for the interpretation of a text? Glen Morgan, writer of *The X-Files* episode 'Blood', states that: 'he doesn't have the slightest clue who or what might have been transmitting the subliminal messages [in this episode] and doesn't really care, leaving such thing for viewers to consider' (ibid.: 168).

Situation number four: What about when two creators of a text contradict each other? The 1960s' British SF programme *The Prisoner* was created by actor Patrick McGoohan and script editor George Markstein. The two men disagree over its interpretation. Markstein says that the lead character in the show was called 'John Drake', and was taken over from another television programme (*Secret Agent*). McGoohan denies this (White and Ali, 1988: 142). Which is the true interpretation?

Situation number five: what if the creator decides that the interpretation made by the viewer is better than their own? Chris Carter again: 'Carter himself acknowledges that he checks out the Internet "almost every day", talking to fans, reading the more thoughtful comments, and sometimes thinking "Hey, they're right . . ."' (Lowry, 1995: 242).

We have plenty of evidence, then, that texts are interpreted in different ways by members of varying sense-making communities. To decide that one of these interpretations is simply 'the correct one' takes us back to a realist mode of making sense of culture. By contrast, the post-structuralist mode that I'm pushing insists that it's the variety of different ways of making sense of texts, of making sense of the world, that's of interest: not the attempt to judge which of them is the correct one.

Once again, this isn't the only methodology that we can use for analysing texts. For researchers who use psychoanalytic approaches, for example, the variety of interpretations which might be made of a text are less interesting and less important than the interpretations they can make using psychoanalytic theory. This is also true for many Marxist writers. But these structuralist approaches aren't the focus of this short book.

Does that mean that anything goes? That I can just come up with any interpretation of a text that I want?

Absolutely not. As I said in Chapter 2, there are always limited numbers of reasonable interpretations available in a given culture at a given time. If you're the only person who makes an interpretation, then it's going to be seen as madness. We need to have evidence that particular interpretations are reasonable. That evidence consists of other texts that make it clear that other people might have made such an interpretation – that you haven't imposed a reading on a text where nobody else would see it. Doing textual analysis means making an educated guess at some of the most likely interpretations that might be made of a text. Our research can show us the limits of what might be likely.

These will sometimes surprise us. For example, I was surprised to discover that for some viewers of the British children's programme *Teletubbies*, there was a strong sexual message. Now to many viewers – including, I would guess, members of its largest audience of pre-school children – this programme appears to be about four sexless, colourful creatures, with the large eyes and overlarge bellies of babies, engaging in banal and repetitive everyday domestic life in a super-modern house under a hill. But the interpretation of this text made by the American tele-evangelist Jerry Falwell is quite different. This viewer has gone on record to publicly condemn the show for 'promoting homosexuality':

> The sexual preference of Tinky-Winky . . . has been the subject of debate since the series premiered in England in 1997. The character, whose voice is obviously that of a boy, has been found carrying a red purse in many episodes . . .Now, further evidence that the creators of the series intend for Tinky-Winky to be a gay role model have surfaced. He is purple – the colour of gay pride – and his antenna is shaped like a triangle – the gay pride symbol. (quoted in Wilson, 2000: 18)

Jerry Falwell's interpretation of the programme borders on the grounds of what we call 'madness' but it's obviously sensible within a certain sense-making community (born-again Christians in the USA), who, if they didn't interpret the programme in that way before they read Falwell's pronouncement, will certainly be looking for evidence of this tendency when they now return to the texts. By his very pronouncements, Falwell has made such an interpretation a more reasonable one for a given community, which is what is interesting, for textual analysis.

This goes against a tendency in some other disciplines, where creating very original and clever interpretations of familiar texts is a worthwhile pursuit (again, this is part of the function served by a training in English Literature or Film Studies). And it should be borne in mind, as I argued in the last chapter, that for those researchers who are politically active and wish to intervene in sense-making practices as a political act, attempting to disseminate alternative reading strategies may be a useful thing to do. But ultimately, in trying to understand processes of sense-making, we should be looking for evidence of reasonable interpretations of texts, which will be multiple, but are never completely open or arbitrary.

How do we decide which texts to analyse?

This is one question that I can't answer in a straightforward way. What I *can* say is that you always have to start with a question. It is because we are interested in finding out the answers to particular questions that we choose texts, and then perform textual analysis on them. When you know what your question is, you can start researching to find suitable texts to analyse.

Because of the way that Humanities disciplines in universities operate, research is often valued when it's original and creative. I can't describe how to think of original questions to ask about culture. But I can suggest the *kind* of questions that have traditionally been important for the disciplines that use textual analysis: and most of these questions are linked by a concern with *politics* (in the widest sense of that word).

Media studies has mostly been interested in how the media represent traditional forms of politics. So the most common texts for study in that discipline have been non-fictional ones – newspapers, television and radio news, current affairs and documentaries. The questions asked of those texts have been: How well do they cover traditional politics? How accurate or how biased are they? How well do they inform citizens? Media studies has also moved into identity politics. The term 'identity politics' refers to the idea that a single political position can't represent the needs of all citizens equally, that different groups might have different political needs. The first identifiable identity politics in Western countries would be the emergence of the Labour movement in the nineteenth century – a group of people with an identity in common (working class) band together to represent themselves politically, feeling that other politicians (here, aristocrats) don't adequately understand or address their political needs. Other groups that have emerged as identities with politics in Western countries include women (beginning in a recognizable form with suffragists in the nineteenth century), Black citizens of predominantly white countries (with Black civil rights movements in the USA in the mid-twentieth century), gay men and lesbians (in the late 1960s); and an exponentially increasing number of groups in recent times (see Chapter 2). For media studies, questions have been asked about how well media texts represent these groups. Again, news genres are studied for this, as well as entertainment genres such as soap operas.

Mass communications has been similarly interested in politics, but has tended to remain at the level of traditional national politics. Similar questions about bias, accuracy and information are asked: a popular subgenre of mass communication analysis studies televised debates between politicians. But this discipline has another important area of interest – the 'effects' of media texts on large audiences. Questions posed by such research include: What effect will this violent television programme have on its viewers? What effect will this sexualized representation of a woman have on its viewers? (Gauntlett, 1998).

Cultural studies uses the word 'politics' as its guiding concern, in a wider sense than either media studies or mass communications do. Feminist thinking has insisted that 'the personal is political' – that the ways in which domestic relationships are organized is a political one, for example:

> 'Can the relationship between the sexes be viewed in a political light at all?' The answer depends on how one defines politics. This essay does not define political as that relatively narrow and exclusive world of meetings, chairmen and parties. The term 'politics' shall refer to power-structured relationships, arrangements whereby one group of persons are controlled by another. (Millett, 1970: 124)

Cultural studies' research has traditionally had Marxist concerns at its base, in approaching this wider kind of 'politics' – analysing how culture represents the wishes of the bourgeoisie, and teaches the working classes to think that capitalism is good for them, when in fact it's not. All aspects of culture can be analysed for answers to such a question, including news and current affairs, but also soap operas and other forms of drama, light entertainment, reality television, popular novels, and so on. Identity politics has also become important for cultural studies researchers, looking, again, at how these groups are represented. But for a post-structuralist cultural studies, the number of possible questions that can be asked increases greatly. All aspects of culture, in all countries and all time periods, are potentially interesting for research. We can start to ask, how does journalism make it possible to think about 'society' at all? How do talk shows contribute to spirituality? Is Elvis a kind of god? How have fridges contributed to the invention of suburbia? And so on, and so forth.

This quick sketch gives you some idea of the traditional questions and objects of study to which textual analysis can be applied. But as the interests of cultural studies expand to include religion, workplace practice, interpersonal communication and many other cultural sites, it becomes impossible to set the limits on the questions that can be asked. Textual analysis is, ultimately, a methodology within the Humanities. It relies on messy concepts like originality, creativity and inspiration, on researchers living in, or studying cultures, and seeing what they think are interesting aspects of that culture. Things stand out. Ideas occur that the researcher thinks are interesting about the way in which sense-making practices occur in that culture; he or she notices texts that provide evidence about those practices. It may be best, as a new student, to begin your practice of textual analysis with familiar questions about politics and power – how is this group represented, how do these texts work in political fashion? But as you stop being a Beginner, and start becoming an Expert at textual analysis, hopefully you'll begin to develop your own questions, and see interesting new aspects of culture that make you think about questions of sense-making and politics in new ways. Then you can begin to research them.

Important: never say 'I'm going to analyse this text', full stop. That doesn't make any sense. You have to say what you are going to analyse it *for*. 'I am going to analyse this text in order to see how it represents women'; 'I am going to analyse this text in order to understand what it says about free will in a modern society' or whatever. You can never just 'analyse a text'. We analyse in order to answer specific questions.

For example, you might study an episode of *Buffy the Vampire Slayer* in order to understand how it represents women as warriors. Your analysis of the text would then focus on the female characters in the text, how they are presented, perhaps, in relation to previous female leads in American drama series, how they dress, other, move, speak, take control of the narrative, and would choose a number of elements from the text that ar your interest, and try to make sense of them in ways which would be likely interpretations.

But supposing you were interested in a different question, say, the way in which our ideas about identity and choice function in late capitalist society. We know from historians that before the nineteenth century in Western cultures, expectations existed that everyone was born into a certain role in society (peasant, aristocrat, royalty) and that there was no expectation that anybody would be able to change that role (that's why some of us have inherited surnames that tell us our jobs – Mr Baker, Ms Carter, Dr Smith). In late capitalist society, ideas about roles in society have changed to the point where we now expect to have the right to choose our own career paths, marriage partners and trajectories in society. If you were interested in looking at this aspect of sense-making, then *Buffy* would again be an interesting text. This time you would analyse the relationship between Buffy and Giles, her 'watcher', the authority figure who is constantly telling her that it's her destiny to be a vampire slayer, that she can't escape it, she can't just go shopping, or do what she wants and be a 'normal' girl (a 'feudal' view of the world). You would study Buffy's responses to this, how they function in the overall narrative, and so on. Again, you'd have to make sense of these elements of the text in ways that aimed for likely inter-pretations but it would be different elements of the text that you would choose to study.

What we don't do in this kind of post-structuralist textual analysis is try to, or claim to, study 'the text in itself', looking at all of its elements as a self-contained work of art. This is another point where this form of textual analysis differs from the kind employed in traditional English Literature or Film Studies. Those approaches to the analysis of texts want to understand the texts they study as perfectly formed works of art – therefore, every element of them should be studied, because it will all add to the overall understanding ('appreciation') of the text. It's not acceptable just to pick out the bits that interest you and talk about them. This 'whole work of art' theory of the text is described by David Bordwell and Kristin Thompson:

> If you're listening closely to a song on a tape and the tape is abruptly switched off, you're likely to feel frustrated. If you start reading a novel, become engrossed in it, and then misplace the book, you will probably feel the same way. Such feelings arise because our experience of artworks is patterned and structured. The human mind craves form. For this reason, form is of central importance to any artwork, regardless of its medium . . . by film form . . . we mean the overall system of

relations that we can perceive among the elements of the whole film . . .
we should strive to make our interpretations [of films] precise by seeing
how each film's thematic meanings are suggesting by the film's total
system. (1997: 65, 66)

It seems obvious to me that these writers are wrong. They might
think that people *should* consume texts only as complete wholes but
we know that in everyday life, most people *don't*. We catch bits of
songs on the radio, flick in and out of television programmes, read
some bits of some articles in magazines, miss bits of films because
we're turning to the people in the row behind us and telling them to
keep their bloody kids *quiet* and so on. But for this traditional Literature or Film Studies, we should never attempt interpretations of texts
('works of art') unless we draw on information about every element
of the text – the 'total system'. This 'close reading' approach to
interpretation is, like the validation of the author's interpretation of
texts described above, a prescriptive one, rather than a descriptive
one. Bordwell and Thompson's method of making sense of texts is
only one, very limited approach: what we might call the *scholarly*
mode of engagement, the province of academics and fans. There's
nothing wrong with taking this approach if we want to understand
how these texts function for fans or for academics but it's only one
subset of a much wider set of interpretive processes. Post-structuralist
textual analysis is more interested in trying to recover information
about practices of sense-making in culture more generally so there is
no need to study every element of every text for every question.
Rather, you need to pick out the bits of the text that, based on your
knowledge of the culture within which it's circulated, appear to you
to be relevant to the question you're studying.

You could waste thousands of words analysing every element of
every text you study – every piece of dialogue, every hairstyle, bit of
make-up, clothing, movement, tone of voice, lighting, colour choice,
shot, piece of editing, and so on – but most of the information that
you generate would be completely uesless. All texts have some
elements that are more important than others; and not all of the
elements you analyse might bear any relation to questions that you
are trying to answer. I saw an episode of the American action series
JAG (set in a military court) while I was writing this chapter, and
started watching the walls in the show – looking at the incidental
detail in the background of the set. The scene was a military briefing,
they were in a room that was institutional and unremarkable – beige
walls, flat lighting. Obviously these elements of the set design had

some significance to the viewer – they gave the scene a certain tone. They weren't wood panelling – so it wasn't meant to be a rich and upper-class home they were in. They weren't clinically white and gleaming – so it wasn't a hi-tech scientific or medical institution. But there were also minor details – a whiteboard in the background with a red and white strip across the top, some scribbled notes, a poster on the back wall . . . If you started performing a textual analysis on every single one of these elements, as though they were all as important as the character who was framed and in focus in the middle of the screen giving vital plot information, then you would be moving further away from likely interpretations of the text. This is not how *JAG* – from my knowledge of TV action series, and of *JAG* itself – is watched.

This brings us back to the point made above – the questions you ask are the essential starting point for any textual analysis. Although it makes sense in English Literature or Film Studies just to say, 'Analyse this text', it doesn't make sense for post-structural textual analysis. Indeed, there is a hidden phrase in the instruction 'Analyse this text' in Literature and Film Studies: it's actually demanding, 'Analyse this text [as a work of art, showing how every element of it works together to get across the message and/or effects the creator intended.]' This is not a question that is traditionally addressed by the post-structuralist textual analysis I am describing in this book. Your question is your starting point; and it's perfectly acceptable to discuss only the parts of the text that seem to you to be most important or interesting for answering that question.

Case study

Will Brooker (2000) '1954: censorship and queer readings', in his *Batman Unmasked: Analyzing a Cultural Icon*. London and New York: Continuum, pp. 101–70.

Will Brooker is interested in what might be reasonable interpretations of *Batman* comics in the 1950s. In particular he asks, are Batman and Robin gay? Or, more precisely, who has interpreted Batman and Robin as being gay, how did such interpretations of the comics come to seem reasonable, and how did they circulate in 1950s' America?

Brooker examines a number of 1950s' *Batman* comics that seem to him, as a young heterosexual academic in the twenty-first century, to offer the possibility of a queer interpretation. The foundation for such interpretations is the domestic bliss and emotional closeness of Batman and Robin – or rather, their real-world counterparts, Bruce Wayne and Dick Grayson – as they live together in Wayne Manor.

> Bruce and Dick . . . went out together during the day to combat villains, then came home for a cosy supper and a glass of milk before retiring to bed, and rising for the newspapers over breakfast . . . Take as just one instance 'The Man Who Stole the Joker's Jokes', a story from 1951. The narrative opens with Bruce and Dick at home in Wayne Manor, reclining on the sofa. Bruce is . . . wearing a gown as he reads the newspaper and Dick watches the television. The scene speaks of a relaxed, intimate bonding between two men. (ibid.: 134, 5)

Indeed, Brooker points out that throughout the narratives of these comics, it is threats to Robin which always prove to be Batman's undoing. Robin plays the role traditionally assigned to the love interest/heroine in the adventure genre: he is kidnapped and threatened by the criminals in order to keep Batman out of their way. At one point when Robin is kidnapped, and Batman is asked what he will do, he responds: 'The only thing I can do – surrender! I'd do anything for that kid!' (ibid.: 135); meanwhile he paces the Batcave, the caption reading: 'a distraught and lonely figure' (ibid.: 135). 'Indeed, the storytelling comes intriguingly close to the conventions of the romance comic. Batman and Robin are often framed together in tight close-up, with the emphasis on distraught facial expression and emotion instead of action' (ibid.).

Brooker goes so far as to suggest that the closeness between these characters is worked out as a queer version of *Romeo and Juliet* in 'The Death Cheaters of Gotham City' (1952). Here, Batman takes his own death through poison – and Dick 'despairs' as he crouches over the 'dead' body (ibid.: 139). Brooker also notes that stories such as that in *Detective* #190, December 1952, end with Robin saved from the villains and: 'a circular vignette of Batman with his arm around Robin in mid-shot' (ibid.: 140). Here Brooker analyses the visual elements of the text as well as the written words. The image needs to be interpreted as much as words do.

By drawing together this textual evidence, Brooker shows that it's certainly *possible* to interpret the relationship between Batman and Robin as a sexual one. But is it *reasonable* to do so? In particular, is it reasonable to think that comic strip readers in the 1950s would have been likely to make such interpretations? Brooker insists that it is because he has found evidence that this is precisely how some readers in the 1950s *did* interpret these *Batman* comic strips.

The idea that Batman and Robin are gay is introduced to public discourse in 1955 by a medical doctor – Fredric Wertham – concerned about the effects of such a representation on impressionable youth (it might turn them gay), in his hugely successful book *The Seduction of the Innocent*:

> At home they live an idyllic life. They are Bruce Wayne and 'Dick' Grayson. Bruce Wayne is described as a 'socialite' and the official relationship is that Dick is Bruce's ward. They live in sumptuous quarters with beautiful flowers in large vases, and have a butler, Alfred. Bruce is sometimes shown in a dressing gown. As they sit by the fireplace the young boy sometimes worries about his partner . . . it's like a wish dream of two homosexuals living together. (Wertham, 1955; quoted in Brooker, 2000: 103)

Wertham himself reaches this conclusion because the young gay men that he has been working with (trying to cure them of their homosexuality) have told them that this is exactly how they interpret these comic books: 'I felt I'd like to be loved by someone like Batman' (ibid.: 141):

> One young homosexual during psychotherapy brought us a copy of *Detective Comics* with a Batman story. He pointed out a picture of 'The Home of Bruce and Dick', a house beautifully landscaped, warmly lighted and showing a devoted pair side by side, looking out of a picture window. When he was eight this boy had realized from fantasies about comic book pictures that he was aroused by men . . . 'I think I put myself in the position of Robin. I did want to have relations with Batman'. (Wertham, 1955; quoted, in Brooker, 2000: 125–6)

Brooker points out a number of elements of public discourse at the time that might have made such interpretations more likely. In the 1950s, he argues, homosexuality was becoming a topic of public discussion for the first time, even if it was in highly coded and circumscribed ways. Psychiatrists were common figures in *Time* magazine, the *Reader's Guide* and other popular journals (ibid.: 118), discussing 'youth' problems: effeminacy, the man's role, homosexuality, the nuclear family and juvenile delinquency (ibid.: 111). The images of homosexuality that Wertham relies on in order to argue that Batman and Robin are gay – their good taste, their expensive clothes – were precisely those that were being offered up as facts to the public at the time. For example, Brooker quotes a US Government document from the 1950s which advises that male homosexuals could be spotted because they were effeminate 'in manner and appearance', and became 'hairdressers, interior designers, that sort of thing' (ibid.: 128). One gay man recalls growing up in the 1950s, when he had to pretend to be straight – 'I was afraid of revealing my homosexuality by showing the slightest interest in colour schemes and the like' (ibid.: 129).

Similarly, Brooker points out that in the 1950s in America, gay men had to be secret about their identities – pretending to be straight, even to the point of having false names in their queer communities (ibid.: 137). They wore a metaphorical 'mask' (ibid.: 136–7), as one gay man describes that period. This was necessary because of the fear of losing their jobs, being locked up as criminals or diagnosed as mentally ill. In such a context, the story of two men with secret identities living together could be a suggestive one. In a country where homosexuality was still illegal, the communication of homosexuality – for example, when a man was trying to pick up another man by working out whether he was gay or not – had to be done by secret codes and conventions (ibid.: 130). The fact that Batman never says he is gay is no problem for this interpretation – in the 1950s in the USA no gay man would ever dare to say such a thing, in public at least. He would communicate it in a more subtle way, by wearing a particular piece of clothing, perhaps. Brooker suggests that the reading of Batman and Robin as gay may have been reasonable for gay men at the time but not at all obvious for straight readers (which is just how the gay subculture worked to communicate with others).

It's worth emphasizing again the importance of trying to find evidence to work out what might be likely interpretations of a text at a given time. Reading these comics now, when the age of consent for gay men in many states in the UK and the USA, and across Britain, is sixteen years old, where homosexuality is not illegal in most of the USA (but, hello, Alabama, Idaho and North and South Carolina) and nowhere in Britain or Australia – where it has even been taken off the American Psychiatric Association's list of mental illnesses – the idea of living a life in terror of being discovered to be homosexual may seem strange. But we can find texts that suggest that this is an important part of the context for interpreting these *Batman* comics.

Of course, Brooker insists, this is not the only possible interpretation of the relationship between Batman and Robin: he cites other fans of the comics who become extremely angry at such suggestions: 'BATMAN GAY? I DON'T THINK SO . . . LOOK AT THE EVIDENCE . . . it's total BOLLOCKS' (ibid.: 104). And it's not, importantly for this chapter, the *correct* interpretation of these texts. Indeed, if we were to follow the traditional literary approach and ask the author, then it's clear that it's a 'wrong' interpretation: 'Bob Kane [creator of Batman] has dismissed the notion of Batman and Robin as homosexuals, aghast that anyone would read into his characters some subliminal ode to homoeroticism' (Vaz, quoted in Brooker, 2000: 106).

So this interpretation is wrong but it's also very real. It was real for the gay men who found in these comic strips some pleasure, and a space for fantasy and identity in a culture that continually pathologized them. It was real for Wertham, the doctor who was so worried that these comics could turn boys gay that he had to publish a book about it. It was real, indeed, to the US government, who became so worried about the public discussion of Batman and Robin's sexuality that they legislated against it: establishing a new 'Comics Code' which insisted, among other things that 'Sex perversion [a contemporary synonym for homosexuality] or any inference [sic] to same is strictly forbidden' (ibid.: 144). This is not the correct interpretation, and it's not the author's interpretation but if we want to understand practices of sense-making then we have to acknowledge that the reading of Batman and Robin as a gay couple is both a very real, and a very important interpretation of these texts.

And the main points again

1   We can never just describe a text, because every description is an interpretation, there are always many possible description/ interpretations of each text.
2   But there isn't an infinite number of reasonable interpretations of any given text at a given time in a given place.
3   When we produce an interpretation of a text, we have to put it into a context – whose interpretation are we guessing at? People reading it when it was first circulated? Or people reading it now? In England? Or in traditional Australian Indigenous communities?
4   For this methodology, none of these intepretations is the single correct one. We are interested in finding out what interpretations people are *likely* to make of texts: not what interpretations we think they *should* make.
5   It doesn't really matter what the creator of the text thinks is the correct interpretation (with one exception: when we can find evidence that audiences actually use that information themselves to interpret the text).
6   You should begin your analysis of a text by making clear what question you are trying to answer.
7   It's fine just to pick out the most interesting and relevant parts of a text for analysis: in fact, this is the correct approach for post-structuralist textual analysis.

Questions and exercises

1   The Internet is a great way to find information, particularly from different countries (Just remember that most websites have no controls over what is put up, so you are just as likely to find the most extreme and unrepresentative forms of sense-making – i.e. 'madness' – as you are to find scholarly work that has been checked by experts in the area to ensure that it fits in with what are generally held to be 'facts'). Using Google (www.google.com), do a search for reviews and discussions from a number of countries of one Hollywood film. Compare and contrast these. What elements of the text do the reviewers agree on? (not just evaluative comments about what is good and bad but descriptive

elements about what is actually in the film). What things do they disagree about?

2 What examples can you think of where the author's interpretation of a text has become common public knowledge? (*Ally McBeal*, for example, David E. Kelley was often interviewed in magazines about the show).

3 Watch one episode of a drama programme on television. Make a list of the most irrelevant pieces of information in the text. Conversely, what are the most important elements of the text for you?

4 In your country, what do you think are the most important questions about culture just now? What do you wish were different about the culture? What texts most interest you? How important are they in the wider culture?

5 Go to the American Christian movie guide at http://www.movieguide.org/?Playing Read the reviews of films that you have recently seen. What have the reviewers seen in the film that you did not see? Then go to the 'Feminist film reviews' site at http://www.mith2.umd.edu/WomensStudies/FilmReviews/. Read the reviews of films that you have seen. What have the reviewers seen in the film that you did not see?

Textual analysis project

1 Write down some topics about culture and how people make sense of the world that interest you.

2 Focus your question to become more specific.

3 List the texts that are relevant to your question from your own experience.

4 Find more texts by doing research, both academic and popular.

5 Find relevant intertexts.

This is the part of your research project where you most need to rely on your expert knowledge of the culture that you're studying. There's no centralized database that keeps track of every text that is produced in every nation, and cross-references it to every other text that is relevant. If you're interested in 'How do lad mags teach their readers to be men?', then as well as the lad mags themselves you need to understand how they fit into culture more generally. You need to know generically how magazines are used – so you might want to look at some other magazines in different genres to see how they compare (try some women's magazines, like *Cosmopolitan*, for example; or some pornographic magazines aimed at men; or other kinds of men's magazines – car mags, perhaps). But you also want to see how these lad mags are being positioned into culture, so texts from newspapers or other sites that discuss these lad mags will give you a sense of what are reasonable positions to take in discussing them. And other sites in culture where masculinity is discussed and taught might be relevant, so look at DIY programmes, or televised sport, perhaps. This can't be a scientific process. No two researchers will come up with exactly the same list of relevant intertexts. And the more familiar you are with the culture you're studying, the more reasonable your choice of intertexts will seem to the people who actually consume these texts.

6   Gather the texts.

This is often the hardest bit of the project, as so few genres of text are actually kept systematically by libraries or archives (see Chapter 4). In Australia and Britain, the national libraries remain useful places for finding popular, as well as academic, books. Films and television programmes can be found through the national archive Screensound in Australia (http://www.screensound. gov.au/index.html); the British Film Institute in the UK (http:// www.bfi.org.uk/); and the American Film Institute (http://www. afi.com/) and the Museum of Radio and Television (http:// www.mtr.org/) in the USA. University libraries are also invaluable resources. It's also worth contacting television production companies directly: with a little friendly persuasion, some of them can be persuaded to allow researchers access to their own archives. For old magazines, access is haphazard. Some libraries have some issues of some magazines; you might find useful older copies in second-hand bookstores, often very cheaply. There's no harm in contacting the publishers directly and asking for access to their archive: the worst that can happen is that they say no. For texts associated with particular organizations – newsletters of a group, for example – you're best just to contact them directly and ask for access.

How do I know what's a likely interpretation? 4

If we're interested in likely interpretations of these texts, why don't we just interview audience members and ask them what interpretations they make?

If we want to understand the likely interpretations of texts, and gather information about people's sense-making practices, why don't we just go out and interview audience members? We could ask them how they interpret the texts, and then we wouldn't have to make any guesses about it – even educated ones.

⌐Audience research¬can sometimes be very useful. It can tell us surprising things about how audiences interpret texts. For example, Henry Jenkins discovered in his work with *Star Trek* fans that a subgroup of female audience members thought that the relationship between Captain Kirk and Mr Spock had a powerful erotic undertone, and interpreted the films and episodes of the television programme in light of this sexual relationship between the two men:

> Kirk and Spock are stranded on a desert planet with little chance of immediate rescue; the Enterprise is away on an emergency mission delivering plague serum when Spock prematurely enters Pon Farr, the Vulcan mating fever. Spock will die if he doesn't achieve immediate sexual release. Kirk comes to the slow, reluctant realisation that the only way to save his friend's life may be to become his sexual partner. Kirk reassured himself, 'No one is asking you to enjoy yourself'. It seemed the logical thing to do at the time. (quoted in Jenkins, 1992: 185–6)

However, despite these unexpected insights, audience r/ also have practical and theoretical drawbacks.

In practical terms, the biggest problem is that it's exp/ can be cumbersome. If the audience's responses are no/

boxes (see Chapter 5 on content analysis), then it takes a lot of time to interview a large number of audience members – either individually or in focus groups – and to transcribe this data.

The fact that this is a lot of work would not, in itself, be a reason to avoid audience research if it weren't for a second, theoretical, problem. Audience research sometimes claims to find 'the reality' of the interpretations made by audiences (see Ang, 1985: 11; McKee, 1999). But this isn't exactly the case – at least, not in the way it's often understood. Audience research actually produces more texts – tables, statistics, articles, books and newspaper stories. It doesn't produce 'reality' – it produces representations of reality. And just like any other texts, these tables, statistics, articles, books and newspaper stories also have to be interpreted. Just because people *say* when you ask them that *this* is what they think about a particular text, it doesn't mean that this is what it means to them in their everyday lives. This isn't to say that they're lying: it's just that the very process of telling somebody what you think about something isn't the same thing as thinking about it in your everyday life.

First, an audience member might never actually have thought about, or actively made sense of, a text before they're asked about it. Dutch researcher Joke Hermes discovered this when she researched the ways in which women used women's magazines (1995). She wanted to know whether the representations of traditional femininity in these magazines had any impact on their readers. What she discovered was that many of the readers didn't actually make *any* sense of these texts. They consumed them in a distracted way, flicking through them as an activity, but not paying much attention to what they were seeing. Hermes points out that to ask detailed questions about how the readers interpreted these texts actually takes us further away from everyday practices of sense-making because that isn't what these texts are *for*. In the first season of the American sitcom *Malcolm in the Middle*, Malcolm's father is very excited when he gets a letter from the phone company: 'They want to know what I think about Call Waiting!' he says proudly to his family. Then he pauses and his face falls as he turns to his wife: '*Do* I think about Call Waiting?' He doesn't – or at least, he doesn't until he gets *asked* about it.

Second, the questions that you ask necessarily restrict the range of reasonable answers that can be given. If you wanted to find out what *Star Trek* viewers thought about the programme, would you actually have thought to ask: 'Have you ever considered that maybe Kirk and Spock might be lovers?' Similarly, a 'yes/no' question in a questionnaire allows no space for a 'maybe' answer. This is dramatized at its most extreme form in an episode of the British sitcom *Yes, Prime Minister* (season 1, episode 2), where the character of Sir Humphrey is demonstrating to his colleague how opinion polls work, using the example of National Service:

> *Sir Humphrey*: You know what happens: nice young lady comes up to you. Obviously you want to create a good impression, you don't want to look a fool, do you? So she starts asking you some questions: Mr. Woolley, are you worried about the number of young people without jobs?
>
> *Bernard Woolley*: Yes.
>
> *Sir Humphrey*: Are you worried about the rise in crime among teenagers?
>
> *Bernard Woolley*: Yes.
>
> *Sir Humphrey*: Do you think there's a lack of discipline in our comprehensive schools?
>
> *Bernard Woolley*: Yes.
>
> *Sir Humphrey*: Do you think young people welcome some authority and leadership in their lives?
>
> *Bernard Woolley*: Yes.
>
> *Sir Humphrey*: Do you think they respond to a challenge?
>
> *Bernard Woolley*: Yes.
>
> *Sir Humphrey*: Would you be in favour of reintroducing National Service?
>
> *Bernard Woolley*: Oh . . . well, I suppose I might be.
>
> *Sir Humphrey*: Yes or no?
>
> *Bernard Woolley*: Yes.
>
> *Sir Humphrey*: Of course you would, Bernard. After all you know you can't say no to that. So they don't mention the first five questions and they publish the last one.
>
> *Bernard Woolley*: Is that really what they do?
>
> *Sir Humphrey*: Well, not the reputable ones no, but there aren't many of those. So alternatively the young lady can get the opposite result.
>
> *Bernard Woolley*: How?
>
> *Sir Humphrey*: Mr. Woolley, are you worried about the danger of war?
>
> *Bernard Woolley*: Yes.
>
> *Sir Humphrey*: Are you worried about the growth of armaments?
>
> *Bernard Woolley*: Yes.
>
> *Sir Humphrey*: Do you think there's a danger in giving young people guns and teaching them how to kill?
>
> *Bernard Woolley*: Yes.
>
> *Sir Humphrey*: Do you think it's wrong to force people to take up arms against their will?
>
> *Bernard Woolley*: Yes.
>
> *Sir Humphrey*: Would you oppose the reintroduction of National Service?
>
> *Bernard Woolley*: Yes.
>
> *Sir Humphrey*: There you are, you see, Bernard. The perfect balanced sample.

Sir Humphrey's example is 'disreputable', but even the most carefully balanced and determinedly objective research faces similar problems. In order to find out audience information, you have to ask questions. And as soon as you ask one question rather than another one, you're limiting the kinds of responses that can be given. There's no way that we can find 'the' single objective question that allows for all possible forms of response equally. I was once surveyed in an attempt by the West Australian government to get information about what the population thought about domestic violence. As it happened, I had just been talking to a friend who had once punched his partner. He was telling me how powerless he had felt at the time, how the partner (whom he had now left) had seemed to enjoy goading him on until he punched him out of frustration. It was a messy, complicated emotional situation. So I was thinking about this when the nice woman on the phone asked me, 'Do you ever think that a woman deserves to be hit by her partner?' I'm sure the research wasn't 'disreputable': but it was closing down the possible ways in which I could offer my thoughts on this question. The very question assumed that women are the only people who suffer from domestic violence but even in heterosexual relationships, this isn't the case. It assumed that only heterosexual people have relationships (in the questioner's fictional example this wasn't a woman being hit by another woman, it was a woman being hit by a man) – again, this isn't always the case (the friend that I'd been talking to had punched his boyfriend). The question assumed, in the use of the word 'deserve', that people who responded in the affirmative were those who thought that hitting somebody was a punishment for bad behaviour, either deserved or not – and my own thinking on the issue was confused precisely by the fact that this isn't always the case.

So I launched into a long, rambling process of thinking out loud, raising these issues with the interviewer, discussing the implications of the various terms, discussing what my friend had said, raising the possibility that sometimes people in relationships might *want* to be hit as a means of actually taking power, not of losing it and so on. She listened very patiently, and when I stumbled to a halt, she asked: 'Shall I put you down as a yes, then?' I wasn't a 'yes'. Eventually I had to go down as a 'no': I don't think people *deserve* to be hit in relationships. I also think it's a lot more complicated than that: but there's no way that was going to appear in this survey. I became one more member of the population who thought that domestic violence was bad. And that was that.

Third, information is always gathered in a relationship. There's somebody or something asking the question (either a researcher, or a questionnaire) and the people surveyed will necessarily give their responses with that in mind. Ellen Seiter describes some audience research she conducted where she became particularly aware of this fact:

> Throughout this interview [with two television viewers] it was uppermost in these men's minds that we were academics. For them it was an honour to talk to us and an opportunity to be heard by people of authority and standing. They made a concerted effort to appear cosmopolitan and sophisticated . . . [they] began the interview with a disclaimer about the amount of time spent viewing . . . This was an unusual start for an interview because Mr Howe had answered a newspaper advertisement asking to interview soap opera viewers . . . [one] then offered an excuse for why they do watch: to see the homes and locations on the shows. (Seiter, 1990: 62, 63)

Often people will emphasize the 'quality' programming that they watch, and denigrate programmes that they actually like ('those soap operas, they're crap') because they think that this is what researchers want to hear (even if it isn't).

There's no way to avoid the presence of *some* kind of relationship in every form of questioning. For example, American researcher Labov, who was interested in the speech patterns and vocabulary of Black Americans, found out that the Black subjects in the study spoke differently depending on who was interviewing them: 'Interviewing of Blacks by Blacks is a significantly different practice, with different effects, from interviewing of Blacks by whites' (Bonney, [1983] 2001: 30). There's no way that you can avoid this issue: you can't find an interviewer who doesn't have any race. And we can't just say that the information gathered by a Black interviewer is the 'truth'; while the information gathered by a white interviewer is simply 'wrong'. Rather, we have to realize that people talk differently depending on whom they're talking to. If I'm explaining what I did last night to my friends, to my mother, or to my boss, I'll speak in different ways to all of them – even though I won't lie to any of them. And none of the stories I tell will be the *only* true version.

These issues relate to the gathering of audience information with interviews, focus groups or questionnaires. Another research methodology is ethnographic work. This approach to audience research is slightly different: taken from anthropology, it requires actually living with people for a period of time and observing their everyday life.

Such work – see, for example, Marie Gillespie's *Television, Ethnicity and Cultural Change* (1995), where the researcher lived for a year with a group of British people of Indian descent, and observed how they used television programmes like *Neighbours* in their lives – can overcome the first point raised above. If a text isn't made sense of in any active way but is simply part of the background of everyday life, then the researcher can see that. But ethnographic research still faces the issue that the information produced is always based on how these people behave in front of a researcher. Even after a period of time, even if the researcher becomes a friend, he or she is still *there* and it's impossible to record how people behave when the researcher is *not* there. To take an obvious example – a couple might spend time in front of a television programme kissing, but they're not likely to do it if a friendly media ethnographer is sitting beside them, smiling and waving a notebook.

And, from a post-structuralist perspective, even this kind of research into audiences relies on trying to make sense of texts. Even when we're sitting with somebody, we're interpreting what they're thinking, not looking at it directly. No matter how long you live with somebody, you never get to see the inside of their head (barring a very unfortunate accident). You still rely on outward signals – what they say, what they wear, how they move their bodies – in order to try and guess (make likely interpretations of) what they mean. Ethnographic work can be invaluable for providing much more evidence about how sense-making practices take place: the amount of information gathered by the ethnographer can ensure that they are able to make very good educated guesses about the sense-making practices of the people they study. But this is still not the same thing as just reflecting reality. It's commonly accepted within anthropology that two researchers can witness the same speech, behaviours, rituals, clothing, and yet they can make different interpretations of what they mean to the culture, and how sense-making practices are taking place.

It's useful, when trying to work out likely interpretations of texts, to look for evidence of how audiences have done this. But face-to-face interviewing or ethnography isn't the only – and not necessarily the best – way to do this. Both Will Brooker (in Chapter 3) and Henry Jenkins (quoted above) provide evidence of likely sense-making strategies for the texts they study. This evidence takes the form of texts that have been publicly circulated by audience members themselves. Just because this is public, rather than gathered in face-to-face interviews, doesn't make it any less real. What publicly circulated texts tell us is the ways in which people discuss, in a variety of places, the texts that they're interested in. We must always bear in mind, of course, that none of these is simply an insight into the reality of their thought processes, any more than interview material is. All of these texts are produced for particular reasons, speaking to particular audiences in particular ways. But perhaps the most interesting aspect of the empirical textual evidence gathered by Brooker and Jenkins is that it's *not* produced in answer to the questions of academics: it stands as evidence of sense-making practices taking place before we begin to research them. These are people who are – to return to *Malcolm in the Middle* – thinking about Call Waiting, and who are willing to tell the world what they think about it.

So we're looking for texts that tell us how audiences interpret programmes?

If we want to understand likely interpretations of texts, then gathering other texts about likely interpretations produced by audience members can be very useful. But it's not only texts written by audience members that can be useful. By studying relevant intertexts – those texts that are explicitly linked to another text – we can get a sense of how texts might be interpreted.

Consumers learn how to make sense of and discuss texts just like learning any other parts of language. So it's often from *public discussion* about culture itself that we pick up the terms we use to make sense of it. Because of this, we often find that audience research can be an expensive and time-consuming way to find out what we already know from our knowledge of the culture we live in.

I did some work entitled 'Images of gay men in the media and the development of self-esteem' (McKee, 2000). I wanted to find out how important television was for young gay men when they were growing up, so I interviewed a number of gay men about their memories of the medium. The strange thing was that I could have predicted exactly what I was going to find out before I even started the project – even though I was careful in my questions not to prompt the interviewees, and asked them deliberately open questions about their memories of television. Most of the men I interviewed complained that they didn't like seeing 'effeminate stereotypes' of gay men on television and they wanted to see more 'positive images' of 'ordinary', 'normal' men. I didn't introduce any of these terms in my questions but I could have predicted that the men I spoke to would use this. This isn't to denigrate them in any way. Quite the opposite – they had learned a vocabulary and range of skills for making sense of texts, just as I had. These ways of interpreting representations of gay men (and other identity groups) are now commonplace in the public sphere. The language of 'stereotypes' and 'positive images' emerges from identity politics, starting in America with books like Donald Bogle's *Toms, Coons, Mulattoes, Mammies and Bucks: An Interpretive History of Blacks in American Film* (1973). Such books helped to popularize this approach to texts, making it commonplace for viewers to ask them-selves which characters are 'negative', to pay attention to which roles are recurring, and to name those roles 'stereotypes'. Other identity groups have employed similar kinds of sense-making. Marjorie Rosen discussed the 'stereotypes' of women in the cinema (1975) and Linda Artel and Susan Wengraf prepared a list of desirable 'positive images' ([1978] 1990). Vito Russo took up the vocabulary for gay men, in his 1981 book *The Celluloid Closet*. Now I rarely meet a student who doesn't already know, from popular culture, that stereotypes are bad, and positive images are good. This is a sense-making practice that we learn from intertexts – from the culture around us – and that we learn to apply to representations of oppressed groups.

This is common in audience research – to discover that audience members draw from publicly available knowledges in order to make sense of texts. This means that if you know what those publicly available knowledges are, then you can make an educated prediction that some audience members will use them to talk about texts. This isn't the same thing as saying that these public discussions 'influ-ence' or have an 'effect' on these viewers. Rather, in the same way that academics read books in order to get information and ideas, so these viewers can consume intertexts for that reason. And, to use the language metaphor again, although we can't predict what any indi-vidual viewer will think or say, we can understand the kinds of approaches that they have at their disposal in discussing such a topic.

Sometimes audience research can actually tell you *less* about the process of sense-making than textual analysis can. This is because as soon as you set the terms of the questions, you have in some ways limited the possible answers. So if I had asked the men in the survey I described above: 'Do you think there should be fewer stereotypes of gay men in the media?', I am certain that I would have had 100 per cent saying 'Yes' – simply because it's public knowledge that stereotypes are bad. But that approach would close down a load of other questions that I could ask with textual analysis, for example, 'Are stereotypes always bad things? Can a stereotype also be a positive image at the same time? Who decides what counts as 'positive' in a positive image?' Audience research can end up simply discovering the same things over and over again – 'stereotypes are bad' – and never getting any further in thinking about the way that texts function.

So we're looking for textual evidence of likely interpretations. Audience research – interviews, focus groups, ethnographic work – can form an important part of that evidence. But it has to be treated like any other text – we have to be careful about how we interpret it – and it doesn't give us a more privileged insight into reality than other relevant, published texts.

Not every academic would agree with this post-structuralist approach to textual analysis, of course. Some media scholars who use ethnography describe it as getting *Back to Reality* (McRobbie, 1997). From their perspective, other forms of data gathering – such as this kind of textual analysis – will always be inferior and less closely tied to reality.

So how do we discover the likely interpretations of a text?

To recap Chapter 3: first, choose your question. When you've found a question that interests you, it's also necessary to identify the texts that you think will be useful in trying to answer that question. Often, these two stages in the research occur at the same time – you come across a text that strikes you as interesting, that makes you think about processes of sense-making in a new way, and leads you on to a research track looking for other relevant texts. For example, an article that I wrote about the ways in which men and women think about their bodies was inspired by seeing an advert in the cinema for the *Godzilla* movie: 'Size does matter!', said the tagline, and the audience laughed. This made me think about why they laughed – what unspoken knowledge did they have that made this line work as a joke? And assuming that it was something about penis size, what did that tell us about the power that men are perceived to hold in culture, given that the penis is so often represented, in feminist writing and in culture more generally, as some kind of weapon? That then led me on to research looking for other texts that drew on discourses of penis size – women's magazines, men's pornographic magazines, health programmes on television, erotic novels for women, and so on.

As the instructions for your 'Textual analysis project' in Chapters 2 and 3 have pointed out, after you have formulated a question about sense-making and its importance, the next stage is to gather as many relevant texts as you can. This is, as I suggested in Chapter 1, your empirical evidence – the traces that are left of sense-making. Obviously, the more you can gather, the stronger your argument will be. This stage of the research can offer practical difficulties – see the instructions for step six of your Textual Analysis Project for some advice about this.

I've got my question; I've got my texts; and now . . .?

I can summarize everything in this section in three words. When you come to make your educated guess about the likely interpretations of a text, bear in mind: context; context; context.

Remember the Warlpiri video. The likely interpretation of that text depends on whether you're looking for the likely interpretations for a Warlpiri viewer, or for a Western viewer. The same thing's true for all texts you analyse. Suppose you're studying the role of music videos in thinking about what is a fashionable and desirable appearance. You have a music clip that shows a young woman with a spiral perm, bright pink shiny lip gloss and blue eyeshadow. How is that video likely to be interpreted by its viewers? If we imagine such a video put into two different contexts, we can guess that it will be interpreted very differently. If we ask how it might have been interpreted by viewers watching it broadcast on *Top of the Pops* or the Australian music programme *Countdown*, in the early 1980s then it's reasonable to guess that it would have seemed to be the height of fashion: viewers would be invited to think of this woman as desirable, or as someone to be imitated. Her hair and make-up would have been offered to the viewer as a possible model for their own bodily practices.

But if exactly the same video clip were played in 2003, it's likely that it would be read differently. If it were played in a nostalgia retrospective programme called *I Love the early 1980s*; or Bob Downe's *Fabulous, Famous and Forgotten*, then exactly those same elements of the text would have to be read as signifying, perhaps, 'the early 80s' as a concept, perhaps nostalgia, camp, certainly objects of humour and derision (although having watched Sophie Ellis Bextor murdering the daaaancefloor, the likely interpretation might be pushed back towards 'fashionable, role model' once again).

This single example is only to illustrate this point: what makes us 'educated', in our 'educated guesses at the likely interpretations of a text', is our knowledge of relevant intertexts: the same ones that audiences have on hand when they interpret that text. I would divide these, for convenience, into four categories – although this is only a rough guide. It's not exhaustive, and they're not really mutually exclusive.

1   Other texts in the series
2   The genre of the text
3   Intertexts about the text itself
4   The wider public context in which a text is circulated.

Other texts in the series
If you want to understand likely interpretations of a television programme, a book in a series, or an issue of a magazine, you must familiarize yourself with several episodes, books or issues. Don't attempt to guess at likely interpretations from your exposure to a single episode, book or issue. This is how mad interpretations are produced.

I learned this lesson when I first saw *Jerry Springer*. In this US talk show, the topics are always outrageous (usually involving unusual sexual combinations or sexual desires), and guests, unlike those in most chat shows, often end up bitchslapping, punching, or throwing chairs at each other. Security guards have to rush on to the stage in each episode and physically restrain the guests from doing serious physical harm to each other.

The first time I saw this programme, I just didn't get it. In fact, I was pretty disturbed by the whole thing. It looked unethical, it looked violent, it looked like these people were breaking all the rules of civilized conduct. It was like nothing I had ever seen before.

But then I watched the programme a few times, and I began to see the structures. The first episode I saw wasn't a one-off aberration where civilization broke down. The guests knew they weren't coming on to talk – they knew what was going on and they were fully expecting to fight. There are rules about when the first chair may be thrown – the fighting usually breaks out just as Jerry finishes introducing the final guest and explaining their situation. The security guards allow very little time for fighting before they come on to break the contestants up, so they can take time out. And then round two begins. What I began to realize was that this wasn't a talk show gone bad – it was a hybrid talk/sports show, and no more violent than a boxing match or a rugby game. These people weren't being tricked into coming onto one kind of show, and then finding themselves in another. They knew what was happening – and what was happening is that they were in a sports event. Just as wrestlers, football players or boxers go into a space where controlled and monitored violence can be conducted for entertainment, so do these guests. The regularity of this series means that guests are unlikely to be caught unawares when they appear on it: its very infamy ensures informed consent on the part of the participants. If I had only seen a single episode, then I wouldn't have known how the programme worked, what viewers can expect of it, and what it is for.

This isn't the same thing as an aesthetic insistence that you have to judge every element of a text against 'the whole work of art'. I'm not saying that if you're writing about, say, *Neighbours* or *The Bold and the Beautiful*, that you have to watch every single episode of them; or that if you want to study *Uncut* or *Q*, then you must read every issue ever published. Quite apart from anything else, it would be impossible in many cases (many episodes of many programmes have never been kept for posterity); and extremely expensive in others (how many researchers would have to work for how many weeks to watch every episode of one of the US's longer-running soap operas?). Rather, I'm saying that you should study enough texts in the series to get a sense of its own rules, and how it works. If you only study one or two issues, books or episodes, you'll have no idea if they are odd examples of the type, or completely typical. If you only saw 'The Body' episode of *Buffy: The Vampire Slayer* (the one where her mother dies), you might come away ready to describe this series as a dark, gritty and harrowing programme about real-life emotional issues. Which of course, it is, but it's also funny and witty and does very clever self-reflexive narratives that parody the genre in which it's set. You wouldn't know that from watching the single episode. And nor would you have any sense of just how *different* that episode is from the rest of the series; nor of the power it might hold for an audience precisely for that reason. It's only by consuming several texts in a series that you get a sense of what the rules are, and what various aspects of it mean. You start to see what is considered as normal in the programme, and what is unusual. You become familiar with the programme's strategies for organizing characters and information, for example, you see that if a character makes it into the title sequence of a soap opera then she is part of the central community, whereas characters who don't are always somewhat on the outer no matter how long-running they might be. Every magazine, book series, programme has its own internal rules in this form: it's only through your familiarity with these texts that they will become familiar to you.

Of course, this doesn't allow us to guess at the likely interpretations made by those people who never watch a show, read the magazine, or the book series, but just happen to flick through it for five minutes, or skim through it in the doctor's waiting room. The responses of such distracted viewers are harder to account for as sense-making practices. They may make no interpretation at all, their minds wandering elsewhere as they turn the pages or flick the channels. Or they may have a very strong reaction which is quite different from that of a regular consumer ('this is soooooooo stupid'). As I suggested above, these kinds of responses are difficult to recover: audience interviews probably wouldn't pick up these consumers either (they may never know the name of the text they hate, or didn't pay attention to). By learning more about the texts in a series, you're more likely to be able to produce an educated guess at the likely interpretations of people who actually *interpret* that text.

The genre of the text
Genre is a powerful tool for making sense of texts. Genres work by providing conventions which allow efficient communication between producers and audiences. If somebody's hit in the face with a frying pan in a *Tom and Jerry* cartoon, we know that this is meant to be funny. We shouldn't worry about whether the character will survive the attack, or whether they'll be disfigured by it. That would be silly. By contrast, if a character is hit in the face with a frying pan in *The Bill* or *Law and Order*, we know that it's a serious assault, that it hurt, and that there will be ramifications in the narrative. Knowing the genre and its rules helps us to make reasonable guesses at how a text is likely to be read by audiences.

Take the example of *Little Shop of Horrors* – a 1986 film about a carnivorous alien that crashes on Earth. The hero is a young man by the name of Seymour Krelborn, who works in a downmarket florist and is in love with a young woman called Audrey. One day he finds a strange plant while walking in Chinatown: taking it back to the shop he discovers that it requires blood in order to grow. It becomes immensely large, until it towers over him, and then it reveals that it can talk. It demands that Seymour brings it more blood, and suggests that he murders the vicious boyfriend of Audrey, who regularly beats her: 'A lot of folk deserve to die . . . it's true, isn't it?'

A disturbing situation for anyone. How would you react? Would you cope, as Seymour does, by bursting into song?

If you want a rationale
It isn't very hard to see, no, no no
Stop and think it over, pal
The guy sure looks like plant food to me.

What is an audience meant to make of this? Why would a character respond to a terrifying situation like this by singing? And how about the fact that as he sings, a rock and roll band can be heard playing in the background? Where did they come from (there's no band in the film)? Is he in some way unhinged? Are we learning something about the character's mental state? Or is it the alien creature – is it perhaps having some kind of effect on his mind?

Of course, these are stupid questions. The answer to why Seymour starts singing is: 'Duh. Because it's a musical.' To suggest that members of the audience would be plagued by the kind of questions listed above, or would start interpreting this scene in these ways, is a mad response. This is what happens in this genre. If you buy a copy of the film, above the title on the cover it even says: 'Hollywood musicals'. And if that isn't enough, when you open the case and remove the tape, the inside cover is filled with pictures of other Hollywood musicals: *A Star is Born, Calamity Jane, Damn Yankees*. By knowing about the genre and how it works, you have a sense of reasonable interpretations to make of elements of the text.

Which isn't to say that, across very different cultures, other interpretations will not flourish. When I first saw a Bollywood musical (*Khoon Bhari Maang – Marriage of Blood*), I would have been hard-pressed to explain a lot of the action, even with subtitles, and even though it's probably common sense within the rules of Bollywood melodrama. It's perfectly possible that for audiences from other cultures, *Little Shop of Horrors* would be impenetrable (although given the massive global circulation of Hollywood films I'm not entirely sure that this is true).

Buffy the Vampire Slayer provides a useful comparison here. In the sixth series episode 'Once more with feeling', the characters suddenly find themselves singing every time they feel an emotion. *Buffy* isn't a musical, and so the fact that they are bursting into song *does* demand an explanation. In a drama series, if someone confronts an emotional dilemma by singing about it then the expert audience realizes that there's a reason for this, and that it will be resolved in the narrative. Even the characters in *Buffy* are aware of their singing, and unhappy about it:

> *Xander*: It's a nightmare. It's a plague . . . I didn't want to be singing things, but they just kept pouring out. And they rhymed . . .

And, of course, in this genre, there *is* a reason: it turns out that Xander has accidentally summoned a musical demon who gets off on watching people sing and dance until they explode. Why are the characters singing? Because it's a musical; or because there's a demon making it happen. Because we know how the genre works, we know how to make sense of these elements of the text.

We can easily multiply examples here: why would someone go down into a cellar by themselves in a horror film? Because it's a horror film. Arnold Schwarzenegger can outrun a nuclear explosion in *Predator* because that's what happens in action films; whereas a nuclear bomb going off in a docudrama like *The Day After* or *Threads* is going to have serious repercussions. And so on.

It's important that you familiarize yourself with the genre of the texts you're analysing to prevent you from making guesses at interpretations that don't work within that genre. It's also important to bear in mind, when you're thinking about what people might actually *do* with texts, that different texts have different kinds of *modality*. The term comes from linguistics: Bob Hodge and David Tripp use it in their book *Children and Television* (1986) to discuss the way that some genres are perceived to be strongly related to reality (such as news, current affairs and documentaries), while others are strongly distanced from it (cartoons, musicals). This distinction is common sense, and part of public debate about media ('escapism', realism, etc.), so we can guess that it contributes to likely interpretations of texts. Texts with a high modality are expected to offer information and ideas that can be applied to other parts of our lives. So a news programme will tell us about, for example, the practices of the current government, and we expect that we can use that information to make a decision when we come to decide which party to vote for. A traffic report is even more directly applicable: we learn a road is busy, we take an alternative route. By contrast, we don't expect to learn life lessons or useful information from a *Tom and Jerry* cartoon. You can't really brew up a potion that will make you super-strong using mothballs and detergent, as one *Tom and Jerry* cartoon suggests. Anybody who actually tried to do it would be employing sense-making practices far outside of the usual consensus: he or she would be, once again, mad.

Intertexts about the text itself

As I mentioned above, you can get a sense of likely interpretations by looking at intertexts – publicly circulated texts that are explicitly linked to the text you're interested in. These might be letters, Internet posts, reviews or articles where viewers describe their own interpretations of the text; or other pieces of entertainment that reference the original text (Burt Bacharach songs turning up in the world of Austin Powers, making clear their status as classic love songs); or we could use wider discussions about how texts in that genre function. Once again, these texts don't simply tell us the truth of how people really interpret these texts, any more than interviewing them about the texts does. And it doesn't mean that audiences simply think what they are told to think in these intertexts. Rather, as in the example of 'stereotypes' discussed above, viewers draw on available ways of thinking about texts in order to make sense of things – just as much as academics do.

One of my PhD students is working on legal television shows. He's interested in what they tell us about the way that people think about the concepts of law and justice in Western countries. Before he could start making confident interpretations of the texts of *The Practice* and John Grisham novels, he had to find evidence that anybody actually interpreted these texts as having anything to do with the law. Maybe the fact that these shows and books have a legal setting is actually quite unimportant to viewers and readers? Perhaps the law is just a backdrop, the scenery against which these stories take place?

Luckily evidence can easily be found that thinking about legal issues is, in fact, part of the pleasure of *The Practice* for its fans. The fan website run by Arthur Tham, for example (http://dekland.tripod. com/thepractice/about-this-site.html) includes a review of each episode written by 'Doug Salvesen, a litigator at the Boston firm of Yurko & Perry', where he assesses the legal issues raised in each episode:

> While the facts of Johnson's killing strongly suggest the lack of intent, there was a much better case for manslaughter. Before the trial, the prosecution had offered a deal which would have required Burnett to plead guilty to manslaughter, but this offer was withdrawn during the trial. In an actual trial, the prosecution would have also charged Burnett with manslaughter, so the jury could have had the option of convicting him of that lesser charge . . .

On another website, a review of *The Practice* distinguishes between it and *Ally McBeal*: 'The hugely popular *Ally McBeal*'s emphasis is one-dimensional – mainly sex and sexual problems . . . By contrast David Kelley's *The Practice* places lawyers' ethics as the central element of the programme' (Ross, 2002).

An interview with David E. Kelley, the creator, producer and head writer of *The Practice*, notes that:

A former lawyer, Kelley likes to deal with the issues of morality and ethics. What might be 'immoral' might be perfectly ethical, especially in the practice of law. His characters are basically moral characters trying to traverse in a world where ethics and morality are at odds with one another – just like most of us. (Patrick, 1999)

And so on. Gathering such textual evidence (and without appealing to the idea of these texts simply being the 'truth' of viewing practices, or of viewers being cultural dupes who believe what they're told to), it seems reasonable to guess that viewers of *The Practice* might actually be thinking about the legal and ethical issues it raises, in a way that, for example, would be less true for the (1997) Michael Richards' slapstick comedy *Trial and Error*.

The wider public context in which a text is circulated

This is the most vague and all-inclusive category of context. We draw on all kinds of other knowledges about how the world is organized – how we make sense of it – when we make sense of a text. Language is an obvious one. We're not taught English at school for the express purpose of employing it later in our lives to understand an episode of *Friends*. But although there's no direct linkage between that show and the storybooks at primary school that brought us to the point where we can understand English, we can still draw on that knowledge in order to make sense of what Phoebe means when she says: 'I'm doing all new material tonight. I have twelve new songs about my mother's suicide, and one about a snowman' ('The one with the monkey'). We know what a snowman is, and that it's often linked to images of childhood, innocent fun and families playing together. We didn't have to become familiar either with *Friends* or with the genre of American sitcoms to work it out. Whereas if we don't have such relevant intertexts, and don't speak English, we're going to find it harder to make sense of the joke.

But beyond such specific knowledge about the meanings of words, we also draw on wider sense-making strategies when we interpret texts. Because what I am describing here is literally, 'everything that's in your head', this section is necessarily the sketchiest of the four groups of intertexts I'm describing. But it's useful to think about the 'discourses' that circulate in a culture.

I argued in Chapter 1 that the presence of cultures with different sense-making strategies doesn't mean that 'anything goes' in terms of making sense of the world: a finite number of sense-making strategies will be circulating in a given culture at any given time about any given element of the world.

A new example: the female orgasm can be thought about in a number of ways. From a clinical perspective, a woman's orgasm might be described as: 'Excitement or violent action in an organ or part, accompanied with turgescence; the height of venereal excitement in coition' (as the *Oxford English Dictionary* so clearly puts it). But within a traditionally masculine culture – like traditional pub culture – a woman's orgasm might be something else: something so unimportant that even if it exists it's not really worth worrying about. This attitude is neatly summed up in the old joke: 'How do you give a woman an orgasm? Who cares?' But in therapeutic discourses, a woman's orgasm might be something else again: the desirable end point not only of sex, but of relationships, a pleasure that one has a right to expect: the equivalent (if one reads the women's magazine *Cosmopolitan*) of a promotion – equally exciting, and equally possible if only one will put in a little hard work and ambition.

Each of these ways of thinking about women's orgasms – each of these 'discourses' about them – is associated with a particular 'institution' (to use the terminology of historian Michel Foucault): medical authority, traditional masculine culture, and therapeutic culture respectively. These discourses aren't free-floating ideas invented by a single person. They come from particular places, and are developed, circulated and supported by groups of people who are both linked into a community in some way, and have some authority to introduce concepts into culture (this is what is meant by 'institutions'). They are some of the numerous, but not infinite, ways of thinking about this particular part of the world. Some of these discourses are more common, more powerful, and less easily challenged than others. These 'dominant discourses' (sometimes also called 'ideologies') appear to be 'common sense' – that's just how things are. Dominant discourses are associated with particular cultures: what appears to be common sense in one may be completely foreign to another. For example, as I suggested in Chapter 2, for many cultural groups in Western countries, it's common sense to insist that there are only two sexes, male and female. This is so obvious that to try to challenge it can lead to one being categorized as 'mad'. But in some parts of India – and in some queer cultures in Western nations – this isn't a dominant discourse. Rather, the dominant discourse within *these* cultures is that nature isn't that simple, and that there are multiple sex roles.

We all live in a variety of sense-making communities. We're informed about the consensus on reasonable and common sense ways to make sense of the world in those communities by a variety of texts that circulate within them. A rough typology might include:

- Household units. Texts we encounter in this community include face-to-face interaction and snide notes stuck to the fridge door.
- Friendship groups. Face-to-face interaction, phone calls, emails, texts.
- Workplace communities. Emails, newsletters, and face-to-face interaction.
- Neighbourhood communities. Local newspapers, newsletters, letter drops and neighbourhood meetings.
- City communities. Local radio, local newspapers, local television news programmes.
- National communities. National radio, national newspapers, national television, films, books, magazines.
- Transnational communities. Primarily television and films, also some books.

In each of these communities, some ways of making sense of the world – some discourses – will be dominant. There's no guarantee that the 'dominant discourses' will be the same in every community of which we're a member – it's common enough to live with contradictory dominant discourses. For example, I live in a country (Australia) in which a lot of the public debate at the national level insists that a woman's place is in the home, having children, but I work in a community (University of Queensland, School of English) where a woman's place is at the top of the promotional hierarchy, where all of our professors are female, a majority of Associate Professors and Senior Lecturers are female, and any attempt to argue that these women should not be in the workplace but at home looking after children would be regarded as so extremely outside of our dominant discourses as to be a form of madness.

I'm leaving the smaller communities to one side here, because this is a generalist book and I'm trying to talk to as large an audience as possible. So I'm not even going to attempt to describe what kinds of dominant discourses you live with in your home, your friendship circle and your workplace. But my educated guess is that, in your national community, you will be familiar with a number of dominant discourses – ways of making sense of the world that seem like common sense, and are very difficult to challenge.

Social organisation, large-scale

1. A strong economy is the most important end point for any society (despite their commonsensical status, all of these dominant discourses can be contested – there are always other ways of thinking about the world. So we could argue that money is less important than how happy people in society are, for example – see the next chapter).

2. Progress is a good thing (but some cultures instead see stability as a good thing).

3. All members of a nation have broadly the same attitudes and characteristics – 'Australians' feel like this, 'British people' think this, 'Americans' do this. (But again, this can easily be challenged – because they demonstrably don't. There's no single element that every single member of any national culture shares.)

4. Everyone should be treated equally. (Although this seems like common sense, it has not been the case for all cultures at all times. Also, the simplicity of this dominant discourse hides the complexity of the social issues it addresses. For example, do we mean that everyone should be treated in exactly the same way – 'It doesn't matter if wheelchair users can't climb the stairs into a library, because they have the same right to climb those stairs if they want to'? Or do we mean that society should be set up so that there's an equality of *outcome* – 'We should install lifts or ramps for wheelchair users so that they can access the library too'?)

5. Refugees deserve to be punished, for queue jumping. (An alternative discourse would suggest that there are no queues that refugees could actually join in their countries of origin, that most turn out to be genuinely in need of help, that it doesn't make sense to victimize people who will go on to become citizens of your own nation; yet another discourse would suggest that human rights are important.)

6. Minorities want special rights. (An alternative discourse suggests that in order to overcome established inequalities it's necessary to provide distinct support structures; another would argue that whenever members of a minority group claim the same privileges already owned by dominant groups, it's seen to be 'special rights', even though it's identical to what dominant groups already have.)

7. Immigrants should take on the dominant culture of the country they move to, otherwise you have 'Balkanization' (a nation breaking up into separate little groups). (Alternatively: immigrants should retain elements of their own culture, because this adds to

the variety and interest of national identity. Neither of these discourses can be 'proved' *per se*.)

8   Everyone has the right to be healthy and to have any medical treatment that they need (a relatively new idea in Western democracies, and one that is turning out to be very expensive for the state).

9   There are two kinds of people in the world – criminals and good upstanding citizens/victims. (This discourse ignores the fact that many good upstanding citizens break the law, but don't see it as breaking the law, for example, speeding or drink driving. These discourses tend to suggest that property offences – burglary and home invasion – are the only *real* crimes. The crimes that *I* commit aren't *really* crimes.)

10 'So-called experts' (also known as 'do-gooders', 'social engineers' and 'ivory tower academics') have no right to speak on social issues. (A discourse which is used to devalue expertise, perhaps because of a growing distrust of groups that were previously dominant authorities – called a 'postmodern' approach to knowledge. But an alternative discourse would ask – does that mean that ignorance is a good qualification for speaking out?)

11 Science is objective and truthful (but, as we'll see in the next chapter, scientists don't believe this).

12 The environment is worth protecting (again, relatively recent, and again simplistic in the variety of debates it covers).

Social organisation, small-scale

1   Everyone should be themselves and follow their dream (a therapeutic discourse most familiar in talk shows and self-help books, that has only become dominant in our generation. It tends to avoid the difficult question of what happens at the limits where one person's dream imposes on other people – should people who love to murder just be true to their murderous desires?)

2   Everyone has the right to do a job they enjoy (again, this is a very recent concept, and it's not yet clear if we can run a workable society based on it: who will manage the sewers?)

3   Different races have different natural characteristics. Black people have better rhythm. (But a scientific position insists that there are no natural lines between races, but racial categories are culturally constructed.)

4   There are only two sexes (very powerful – but again, not simply the truth).

5 It's natural for women to be concerned about their appearance, to shave their legs, pluck their eyebrows, wear make-up, exfoliate, cleanse, tone, pedicure, manicure . . . but not for men. (We can see that this is only one possible discourse by the fact that it's now changing. Men are increasingly being required to do the same – see the new lad mags that tell men to do this in order to get laid.)

6 Men are more rational. Women are more emotional. (This dominant discourse is odd because lots of men aren't rational, and lots of women aren't emotional. We know this, but it doesn't seem to stop the power of this discourse.)

7 The nuclear family is the natural, and best, form of child-rearing. Children deserve (only) two parents. (But in many other cultures, extended families are the norm, where kids are raised by many women and men.)

8 Everyone loves children. Children need to be protected from the dangers of the world, including representations of violence and sex. (Alternative discourses might simply say: No they don't. See Philippe Ariès' book *Centuries of Childhood* [1973] for evidence about this. And consider the fact that the age of consent for heterosexual intercourse in some First World countries – such as Spain – is thirteen years old, Avert, 2002).

9 Money can't buy you happiness (which contradicts the economic discourse at number 1).

Culture and representation

1 There's only one reality. (This is common sense, but also so sloppily expressed as to be almost meaningless. As I have argued throughout this book, it's a messy philosophical point. I'm happy to agree – so long as I can add the caveat, but everybody makes sense of it in different ways.)

2 The biggest problem for television news and current affairs is 'bias' and lack of 'objective' reporting. (My way of thinking about this is that every news story is *always* biased – told from a particular point of view – and can never be any other way. 'Objective' means 'I agree with this'.)

3 A successful sportsperson is a national hero and deserves all the funding and special privileges he or she gets, even though other groups don't. (Alternative discourses would ask, why can't we apply the same reasoning to successful writers or academics? But I would say that, of course.)

4 'Natural' is a good thing (especially in advertising and healthcare. But an alternative approach might ask – what about snake venom, sharks and poisonous plants?)

5 Television is bad for your eyes and rots your brain. (Science tells us that books are worse for your eyes – why don't we worry about that? Who says that television rots your brain?)

6 It's obvious that some kinds of culture are just better than others – such as opera, Shakespeare, classical music, literature and movies with subtitles. (An alternative discourse would say – historically, that idea emerges in the nineteenth century, as the elite groups in society attempt to explain why their tastes are better than the tastes of the working classes. It has no explanatory value outside of that class prejudice.)

None of these dominant discourses of course, are completely unchallenged – not in the national public sphere, and not in the other communities that we might inhabit. But as sense-making practices, all of them have the status of being common sense, and are difficult to challenge. You run the risk of being seen as mad (or, in the favoured language of talkback radio hosts, an 'idiot') if you do challenge them.

Should I be looking for these dominant discourses in the texts that I analyse?

Not necessarily. Dominant discourses change over time: it may be that somebody picking up this book in a decade, or twenty years' time, will find it remarkable that some of these ways of thinking about the world ever held sway. So this should not be used as a shopping list, to tick off against the particular text that you're studying. One of the most dangerous tendencies in textual analysis is to try to prove that everything in culture is bad by forcing every text you study into one of these dominant discourses. Finding 'stereotypes' everywhere you look, even when such an interpretation would not be at all obvious to the people who are making sense of it outside of academic institutions, doesn't really tell us much about the sense-making practices in culture. An awareness of the various levels of dominant discourses present in the cultures where a text circulates is invaluable for making educated guesses at likely interpretations, but bear in mind all the other levels of context that inform sense-making practice as well.

How can I 'research' the dominant discourses that audiences might use to interpret a text?

This level of intertexts is the hardest to research in any traditional sense. It's possible to get some sense of this by reading academic histories and accounts of a culture. If you're doing this, then the more you read the better. Remember that every claim about what 'this society thinks' and 'this culture does' is written from a particular perspective. None of them can tell the whole story. And they're also written within the academic genre, which frequently wants to tell us how bad popular culture is, and finds racism, sexism and homophobia everywhere.

Personally, I feel that the best way to get a sense of the dominant discourses circulating in a culture is to immerse yourself in that culture as much as possible – live there for a while. This makes it very difficult for a Western researcher to view, say, a copy of a Singaporean sitcom and try to make an educated guess about likely interpretations of that text by a Singapore audience, unless they know something about Singaporean culture. You could explain what interpretation *you* as a Western viewer make of the sitcom: but without the kind of contextual information described above, you haven't got much chance of making an educated guess about likely interpretations in Singapore.

Anything else I should know?

Yes. There are a few useful tricks you can use to help you see how sense-making practices are working.

Often it's difficult to see past what's common sense to us, precisely because it is such common sense. These tricks can help to make these invisible discourses more visible. One is looking for examples of exnomination; another is the 'commutation test'; a third is paying attention to structuring absences.

Exnomination
This word comes from the writings of French cultural theorist Roland Barthes. Exnomination means 'outside of naming'. Barthes' point was that dominant groups or ideas in society become so obvious or common sense that they don't have to draw attention to themselves by giving themselves a name. They're just the 'normality', against which everything else can be judged.

An example: on the British cop show *The Bill*, there were two kinds of junior policepeople. Reg Hollis was a 'PC' – a 'Police Constable'. And Polly Page was a 'WPC' – a 'Woman Police Constable'. Why was Polly a 'woman', but Reg was just a 'PC' – not an 'MPC' (Man Police Constable)? Because, of course, the titles were first introduced when all PCs were men. The fact that a man was a policeperson was so normal and obvious that you didn't need to draw attention to it. The fact that a woman was a Police Constable was unusual, notable and worth mentioning. We can see a similar process in the phrase 'male model': this is commonly used to describe men who model, while it's rare to hear Kate Moss described as a 'female model'. Models are female, just as policepeople were male. Anything else is an exception.

Texts like these help us see sense-making practices at work. I used the past tense to describe the characters in *The Bill*, because although the characters of both Polly and Reg have survived into the twenty-first century, the 'WPC' has not. The 'W' has quietly been dropped. Now women and men are both 'Police Constables'. The surprise that a woman could be a policeman (as it were) has gone: sense-making practices have changed, and our analysis of the text can show us that.

My own personal favourite example of exnomination is one where popular culture teaches the concept to its own audience. It occurs in *Friends*: Chandler works out for himself how exnomination functions, while listening to Joey advising Ross on how to cope with a difficult situation:

> *Joey*: Move on. Go to China. Eat Chinese food.
> *Chandler*: Of course, there they just call it 'food'.
> (*Friends*: 'The One Where Rachel Finds Out'; Wild, 1995a: 138)

Commutation test

Also useful for making clear what might be too obvious to see in the organization of textual features is the commutation test. This is a thought experiment where you replace one element of a text with a similar but different part of culture. An obvious example is swapping members of two identity groups between roles in a text. For example, what happens if you swap the male and female roles in the 1995 Hollywood film *Boys on the Side*?

The film concerns three women – Jane, Holly and Robin – who go on the run from the police after accidentally killing Holly's abusive boyfriend. It's a 'comedy/drama' (according to the Internet Movie

Database), and a 'chick flick'. Here's what happens in the scene where the accident takes place.

Jane (Whoopi Goldberg) and Robin (Mary-Louise Parker) have gone to visit Holly (Drew Barrymore). Her partner Nick (Billy Worth) is 'in a mood', and has just smashed up their house looking for some drugs he's lost. 'He has a drink and he gets . . . confused,' Holly says. He storms around the house, throwing things against the walls: 'Maybe if you cleaned up, I'd be able to find my shit!' he yells. When the women try to leave, Nick grabs Holly and pushes her over: 'Think you're going somewhere?' They get into a fight, as Nick punches and slaps the women. Robin calms things down, getting Nick to phone a friend who tells him that he has, in fact, already sold the drugs. But he was drunk at the time that he can't remember where he put the money from the deal. Holly taunts him: 'He always hides it in the same three places. But I'm not telling.' Nick loses his temper again, and begins to throw Holly against the wall. Jane pulls him off – and then Holly grabs a baseball bat and hits him across the back of the head. He falls to the ground. 'What is wrong with you?', shouts Jane. Holly makes a face, and asks: 'Did I hurt him?': it's a comic moment. Jane explains very slowly, 'Of course you hurt him – you hit him with a bat!' Nick is on the floor covered in blood – but the performances suggest that this is something almost comical.

What if this were a film about three men?

One of them lives with a violent drug-dealing woman. The other two go to visit him, but his girlfriend is smashing up the flat and throwing things against the wall: 'Maybe if you cleaned up, I'd be able to find my shit!' she yells at him. When the men try to leave, the girlfriend grabs her partner and throws him to the floor: 'Think you're going somewhere?' They get into a fight, only resolved when one of the men calms her down, and they find out that the girlfriend has already sold her drugs. But she was drunk when she did it and she can't remember where she put the money from the deal. Her boyfriend taunts her: 'She always hides it in the same three places. But I'm not telling.' The girlfriend loses her temper again, and begins to throw the man against the wall. The other man pulls her off – and then he grabs a baseball bat and hits his girlfriend across the back of the head. She falls to the ground. 'What is wrong with you?', shouts the second man. The boyfriend makes a face: 'Did I hurt her?' His friend explains very slowly, 'Of course you hurt her – you hit her with a bat!' The girlfriend is lying on the floor covered in blood . . .

Is this a comical scene?

There are so many things wrong with this second version of the film. The idea that a single woman could take on three men and throw them around is ridiculous. The idea that she would be the drunken drug dealer while her boyfriend is expected to keep the house clean so she can find her stuff is bizarre. The idea of the man taunting his girlfriend sits strangely. Finally, the idea that hitting her across the back of the head with a baseball bat could be a comic moment seems really distasteful – I'm pretty sure this would pull the film out of 'comedy/drama' and very much into 'black comedy'.

We can see by performing such a commutation test that there are norms in film-making about masculine and feminine roles. Women are not supposed to be naturally violent in Western cultures. They are not supposed to be drunken drug dealers. They shouldn't scream at their boyfriends to tidy up the house. And smashing a woman's head in with a baseball bat is a more serious thing than doing it to an abusive boyfriend.

Of course, these representations are only one way of making sense of the world. We know from other areas of culture that many men do experience relationships with abusive women. But we also know that such men are often reluctant to come forward precisely because they are seen as wimps because that isn't how we commonly think about domestic violence, or male/female relationships: 'The first reaction upon hearing about the topic of battered men, for many people, is that of incredulity. Battered husbands are a topic for jokes (such as the cartoon image of a woman chasing her husband with a rolling-pin)' (Gross, 2002).

Similarly, despite generalizations about gender, we know that many women are physically stronger than many men (try putting Lucy Lawless into a brawl with Tony Blair, for example). But still, the commutation test shows us that expectations about how men and women behave insist on gender roles that distribute violent ability according to gender.

Popular culture itself sometimes produces very interesting commutation tests. In public discussion about why a company had produced adverts showing naked men in them, a spokeswoman says: 'if the ads had featured naked women they would have been offensive. The funny thing is when you put a couple of blokes in that position who are well muscled and strong, it's simply a twist which is humorous' (Brook, 2002: 5). This test can also be done with objects and ideas, as well as with people from different identity groups. Kath Albury, for example, tries to understand how we think about our sexual tastes in Western culture by imagining a situation where another bodily function was put in its place. Like sex, eating is also a requirement for human survival, a basic human need, but also something that we take pleasure from, and something that we do when we don't absolutely need to simply because we enjoy it. It's also something that requires a certain kind of etiquette about what is and isn't polite behaviour in public (so no talking with your mouth full). Swapping around these two areas of culture, Albury imagines what it would be like if we treated eating the same way as we treat sex in Western cultures, given that a couple may have tastes for quite different kinds of sexual exploits (say, fetishism, public sex, or any of a wide variety of sexual practices):

> Unlike our tastes in food, revealing our sexual tastes is potentially dangerous. Imagine a couple on their first date. She likes olives, he doesn't. They order a half-and-half pizza, with no need to pry into each other's culinary pasts. He doesn't feel the need to ask her how long she's been eating olives, who first gave them to her and how many of her previous boyfriends liked them too. She doesn't think he's neurotic or phobic because he tried olives a couple of times and didn't like them. And if a couple of olives get onto his half of the pizza, he may well eat them, secure in the knowledge that he probably won't be pressured into eating olives at every meal for the rest of his life. He certainly won't write to a food columnist to ask what it means when a woman really likes olives . . . Yet, when it comes time for the couple to share a sexual meal, the situation is very different. (Albury, 2002: 4)

Structuring absences

Often texts will systematically exclude certain kinds of representations and not draw attention to this. This can make it difficult to spot them, of course, but when someone draws your attention to it, it can become obvious. Like exnomination, this can help us to see what elements of a likely interpretation of a text might be important.

Watching *Ally McBeal*, none of the lawyers ever says: 'Isn't it interesting that all of our clients are well off, rich people?' They might be black or white (they are rarely Hispanic); they might be male or female or even (in one instance) preoperative transsexual. They might be gay or straight or bisexual. But they are always well off.

I'm not the first person to spot the fact that American television programmes tend to have a disproportionate number of middle-class characters, rather than working-class ones (Jhally and Lewis, 1992). Previous research draws my attention to this absence. There are television shows that do have more working-class characters – *Law and Order, NYPD Blue* – but they tend to be the more 'gritty' kinds of series. Although *Ally McBeal* doesn't include any working-class characters, that very fact might be meaningful. The programme links middle-class characters with light, entertaining, slightly silly stories. It seems that, in the American television system, working-class life isn't really silly and entertaining and light. It's gritty and dark and dangerous.

Looking for examples of exnomination, applying commutation tests, and paying attention to structuring absences can be useful in our textual analysis. These tricks can contribute to the methodology of textual analysis by making visible what might otherwise be too obvious to see.

What about deep interpretations, that people don't know they're making?

This post-structuralist version of textual analysis is useful for trying to recover sense-making practices. Other approaches to the analysis of texts are not interested in sense-making – the conscious mind – but in other parts of human experience.

The structuralist approaches that I have mentioned in this book – psychoanalysis and Marxism, for example – are interested in things that can't be known. For psychoanalysis, the object of study is the 'unconscious' – precisely the part of the mind that doesn't make sense in the way that we're used to, and that can't be accessed as our conscious minds can. Marxism uses the idea of 'false consciousness' to suggest that sometimes people's sense-making practices are wrong – they think that they think one thing, but really, at some other level, they think another way.

As I keep saying, the kind of textual analysis I'm describing is only one possible methodology for the study of culture. It is specifically designed to research sense-making. Attempts to discover the ways in which the psyche, or consciousness, works outside of sense-making are going to need different approaches. For an introduction to the application of psychoanalytic approaches to the study of texts, and to Marxist-informed approaches to analysing texts, see Robert C. Allen's edited collection *Channels of Discourse Reassembled* (1992), Chapters 6 and 5 respectively. The other chapters of this book are also useful if you're interested in the variety of approaches that you can take to the analysis of texts, beyond the single methodology I'm talking about here.

Case study

Henry Jenkins (1992) 'Scribbling in the margins: fan readers/fan writers' in his *Textual Poachers: Television Fans and Participatory Culture*. London and New York: Routledge, pp. 152–84.

Henry Jenkins is interested in the power relations between television producers and television fans. He wants to know who controls what are the likely interpretations of particular texts, and why it matters what these interpretations are. Is it the producers who make the texts in the first place, or the consumers who make sense of them who ultimately have control over what interpretations come to be seen as reasonable ones?

He examines this question by describing the way that fans of *Star Trek* rewrite the programme in their own texts, and how these relate to the text of the programme itself. Examining the fan novel *The Weight*, by Leslie Fish, he gathers a large number of other fan texts, as well as his analysis of the television programme itself (an obviously relevant intertext) to show what are likely interpretations of this book.

As I said above, if you want to find out how consumers interpret texts, you can't just open up their heads and find out the truth of what they think. Even by simply asking people, or setting various exercises for them to do based on the text (as Hodge and Tripp (1986) do with groups of schoolchildren), we're still always producing texts that need interpretation. This is particularly obvious when the interpretations that audience members make take the form, not of spoken comments in response to our questions, but material cultural products made by fans themselves: short stories, songs – or even, as in the case of Jenkins' study – full-length novels. This is obviously a fan response to a television text that tells us something about the way that fan is interpreting that text, but it's also, in a very literal and obvious sense, a text that itself needs interpretation.

Jenkins points out that the fan novel *The Weight* had already been in circulation for fifteen years when he came to write about it, and is well known within the *Star Trek* culture he is describing as an important text that bears detailed scrutiny and exegesis (detailed explanation of a text). Jenkins analyses this text to show how it provides a 'compelling critique' of the way that social relations are organized in the *Star Trek* television series (1992: 177): '*The Weight* begins with mild grumbling about bureaucratic incompetence and ends with all of the regular characters verging on open revolt against the Federation.'

From a wide-ranging analysis of fan fiction earlier in his book, Jenkins has already provided us with a framework within which he can interpret of this novel: a list of 'Ten ways' in which fans interpret *Star Trek* by 'rewrit[ing]' the show. This list points out the things that fans change when they produce their own fiction and thus provides an insight into the sense that fans have of what they can and can't change about the texts they're interpreting. 'Recontextualization' is one technique used by fans.

It involves stories that fill in gaps in the television series text and explain things that are not properly addressed by it. 'Expanding the series' timeline' allows fans to write stories before or after the televised narrative. Neither of these strategies involves challenging elements of the original text. 'Refocalization' moves attention to characters who are marginal in the televised text, and can have specifically political motives, for example, focusing on marginal female characters, and exploring their characters and situations in a way that a televised text didn't do, because it always unthinkingly placed men at the centre of the stories. 'Moral realignment' challenges the logic of the initial text by questioning the moral positions they present (in Jenkins' example, making Darth Vader a more sympathetic character, which ironically is exactly what the new *Star Wars* films are doing as well). 'Genre shifting' takes characters and situations from the initial text and moves them into different kinds of stories (from science fiction to romance, for example). 'Crossovers' bring together characters from different programmes. 'Character dislocation' is a 'radical manipulation', where characters are completely moved out of their original context, for example, writing a story about *Xena: Warrior Princess* where Xena is a lawyer in twentieth-century America. 'Personalization' allows fans to put themselves into the text; 'emotional intensification' moves away from narrative to focus on characters' emotional responses; and 'eroticization' introduces sex to texts where it wasn't previously there. These are all 'reasonable' things for fans to do when producing texts which reveal their own response to *Star Trek* texts.

The Weight is a fan novel which is written as a sequel to a short story by another fan author – 'The Sixth Year' by Ed Zdrojewski – in which a time travel experiment by the starship *Enterprise* changes the course of history. When Captain Kirk and his crew return to their own time, they find that the Earth is now a non-technological agrarian society, with no defences against alien invasion. *The Weight* tells the story of Kirk attempting to put time back on the course that he knew. As he analyses this text, Jenkins draws on his knowledge of what such fan fiction is for, in order to argue that this book is likely to be interpreted by its readers as a feminist critique of, and a moral challenge to, the values of the television programme *Star Trek*.

For example, Jenkins points out that a number of the characters in this novel can be interpreted as 'doubles' of the Enterprise crew: 'We're your other selves . . . we're the dark side of yourselves, and you can't lose us or ignore us' (1992: 180). These characters are not literally 'doubles' (as in the 'evil double' episodes of *Star Trek: Deep Space Nine*, for example). But as an example of a generically familiar 'moral realignment', the novel's strategy of providing contrasting characters for each of *Star Trek*'s central figures allows for a political critique: 'Kirk's double is the anarchists' female "coordinator", Jenneth Roantree, whose strength, courage and intelligence make her more than a match for the starship captain. Her nurturing relationship with her community poses a fascinating alternative to his exercise of hierarchical authority' (ibid.: 180).

The novel's narrative, as Jenkins analyses it, challenges the rigid, masculine, militaristic social structures of *Star Trek* the television series, undertaking 'the political transformation of Kirk, from the strict yet benevolent patriarch seen in the aired episodes into a long-haired radical' (ibid.: 183). The novel also challenges the sexism of the Star Fleet on television's *Star Trek* which (at the time) still kept female characters in subsidiary and traditionally feminine roles (receptionist, nurse), and in mini-skirts:

> Uhura sees Roantree as a potential champion who may challenge Star Fleet's sexist treatment of its female officers, and open doors for other women to gain command positions: Uhura conspires with Christine Chapel to convince Roantree to accept a post in Star Fleet. Their scenes together provide nuanced pictures of these two women's responses to the patriarchal attitudes and institutions they encounter in the *Star Trek* universe . . . Uhura explains . . . 'there are no female Starship captains . . . My chances are poor. "Insufficient training and experience", they say – after neatly sliding me into a position where I'm unlikely to get either.' (ibid.: 181–2)

Jenkins' analysis of this novel, staying within the bounds of the 'likely' interpretations made by its audience, finds that it: 'questions [*Star Trek*]'s basic ideological assumptions' (ibid.: 184). Examining the way in which audiences interpret the text of *Star Trek*, Jenkins finds evidence in the archive of sense-making that at least one group of fans – those who read and write fan fiction – interpret *Star Trek* itself as being sexist and presenting an authoritarian version of culture. This isn't simply – and never can be – a case of just finding out the 'reality' of what consumers think about a text. It's one example of that messy, uncertain process of making educated guesses about the ways in which other people make sense of the world.

And the main points again

1   Asking audiences how they interpret texts can provide interesting information, but it's not just the truth of their sense-making practices.
2   We can make educated guesses about likely interpretations of a text by familiarizing ourselves with relevant intertexts.
3   These include:
    (a)   other texts in the series
    (b)   other texts in the genre
    (c)   explicit intertexts
    (d)   dominant discourses in the culture where the text is circulating.

4 Useful tricks for seeing dominant discourses include:
(a) looking for examples of exnomination
(b) performing a commutation test
(c) looking for structuring absences.

Questions and exercises

1 Choose a television programme that you've never seen. Watch one episode and make notes about what surprises you, what it does that you haven't seen other television programmes do before. Watch another episode – does it do these things again? Watch a third episode – were the things that you noticed about the first episode the rules for this programme, or were they exceptions?

2 Is it reasonable for a viewer of *Big Brother* in your country to think that the producers of the show manipulate the footage to tell particular kinds of stories and favour particular kinds of characters? How would you find evidence that this is, or isn't, the case? Find that evidence and answer the question.

3 Choose a favourite film. What genres does it belong to? Watch it again – what rules of that genre do you know? How do you use those when you're making sense of the film?

4 Make a list of dominant discourses that I've missed – statements that it would be very difficult to challenge in your culture without people thinking you were mad. Then do some research (including on the Internet, or going to the library) to find evidence of people who disagree with that dominant discourse. What evidence do they provide to challenge the dominant discourse? If you can find a particularly sensitive social issue, try calling up a talkback radio station and putting the alternative perspective: do you get called an 'idiot'?

5 Make a list of professions that often have a gender label put in front of them (like 'male model'). What kinds of professions are still largely thought to be male? Which ones are still largely thought to be female? Find examples of other identities that are exnominated: how easy is it to find examples of exnomination about race? How do the words 'Black' and 'White' get used in texts? How about sexuality? Can you find any references in news stories to 'straight activists'?

Textual analysis project

1   Write down some topics about culture and how people make sense of the world that interest you.
2   Focus your question to become more specific.
3   List the texts that are relevant to your question from your own experience.
4   Find more texts by doing research, both academic and popular.
5   Find relevant intertexts.
6   Gather the texts.
7   Analyse as many of the texts in the genre as you can, getting some sense of the rules for how they work.

At this stage in the analysis, you want to get a sense of the rules for the central texts. Suppose you're making *FHM* magazine a central object of analysis for answering your question about lad mags and how they teach masculinity. You would notice straight away that the magazine gives a lot of explicit instructions – articles whose titles start with 'How to . . .'. One of the first things that you would want to know is whether these instructions are meant to be taken seriously? When you read through articles like 'How to land a 747', it becomes apparent that they are not serious instructional pieces, and there is no expectation that readers will actually use them as a template to go out and attempt to do what is described. You begin to understand how these particular elements of the text work – making jokes about masculinity. If you are familiar with the culture in which they circulate, you will also recognize that there is a particular kind of masculinity – a very traditional one based on macho behaviour and a fascination with big toys – that the magazine is simultaneously celebrating and mocking.

8   Get as much sense as you can of the wider 'semiosphere' (the 'world of meaning', or cultural context) as you can (read newspapers, magazines, watch as much television, listen to as much music as you can to get some sense of how these texts might fit into the wider context).

If you have been watching the news or reading newspapers, you might have picked up that there is an ongoing 'crisis of masculinity' in Western countries. Stories about boys failing in school, doing worse than girls at university, and so on, may provide a relevant context for thinking about the kinds of masculinity these magazines are constructing. The success of *Men Behaving Badly* might lead you to analyse that programme and use it to make sense of the masculinity of the lad mags. Again, there's no simple equation that can tell you what is relevant in wider culture. Once again, it is your expertise in, and familiarity with, the culture that you're describing that are going to determine whether the cultural sites that seem relevant to you are going to allow you to produce educated guesses at the likely interpretations of the texts.

Reading the magazines themselves will also give you a sense of the kind of other texts – music, films, books, television programmes – that the magazine expects its readers to be interested in. While this won't, of course, match up exactly with what every reader of the magazine consumes, it does give you a rough idea of the kind of culture that a reader of *FHM* might encounter. Viewing, reading and listening to some of these might be useful for getting a sense of the reading practices of *FHM*'s readers.

Can't we make it a bit more scientific? 5

It all sounds a bit vague and subjective; can't we make textual analysis more objective?

Textual analysis is a methodology. But that label could be misleading. The term 'methodology' can have scientific connotations. It can imply a standardized procedure that doesn't require any creativity or originality, a standardized recipe that anybody can follow and come up with the same answers every time. Textual analysis isn't like that. And some people who research culture and sense-making practices don't like it very much – precisely because it isn't a very scientific way to find information. There are two aspects of (post-structuralist) textual analysis that are particularly unscientific. First, it doesn't produce quantitative knowledge (numbers). The likely interpretations that you produce aren't given in terms of percentage likelihoods of how many people will make such an interpretation, nor of numbers of people who have made such an interpretation. And, second, this methodology isn't 'iterable' (repeatable). This is a central aspect of the methodological thinking of many scientists: 'the scientific world doesn't adopt [a theory] until the experiments and observations [proving it] have been repeated by others' (Magee, 1985: 71). But if you gave two researchers the same question ('how are women represented in Western culture?'), and asked them to use textual analysis to answer it, they would produce different answers. Even worse – from a scientific perspective – if you gave two researchers the same group of texts (say, ten issues of a woman's magazine) and asked them to answer the same question, they still wouldn't come up with exactly the same answer. The researchers will draw on their own knowledge of the culture within which the texts circulate as they attempt to guess the likely interpretations of those texts. This methodology is part of the humanities more than the sciences.

There are a couple of reasons that some social scientists dismiss this kind of textual analysis. One is boundary guarding: people from many different university disciplines study culture, and of course there's a tendency to insist that the kind of work that *I* do is the best kind of work in the area. But more than this, we live in Western cultures where 'scientific' modes of knowledge are more highly regarded than other kinds of research. Numerical and repeatable forms of information-gathering have an aura of truth about them that can make their results seem powerful. Even advertisers know this:

> Discover double performance Anti-Wrinkle and Firming Cream
> 1. Anti-Wrinkle Action with Pro Retinol A
> Revitalift smooths your face.
> 89% of women noticed that their skin was smoother.
> 2. Firming action with Par Elastyl
> Revitalift reinforces skin's elasticity.
> 71% of women noticed that their skin was more toned and 75% that their skin was firmer. (*New Woman*, August 1996: 3)

A method for gathering information that is neither numerical nor repeatable – a method like this form of post-structuralist textual analysis, for example – is in a poor position to defend itself as a methodology. Because it's not numerical or scientific, it gets lumbered with another name: 'subjective'.

However, these arguments can be countered. It's possible to argue that this form of post-structuralist textual analysis is a valuable methodology, even though it's not a scientific mode of discovery.

First, even those social scientists who critique 'subjective' textual analysis are willing to admit that scientific methodologies are not the only way to gather information about culture: 'What are your criteria of valid evidence? If it is replicability [that is, iterability] as a means of reproducibility, this would eliminate certain great areas that we've considered knowledge – historic knowledge, for example' (Fairchild, in Coulson and Rogers, 1968: 156). As historian Robert Darnton notes, his mode of gathering evidence about the French Revolution – carefully gathering and analysing historical data – 'may seem too literary to be classified under the [name] of "science" in the English-speaking world' (Darnton, 1985: 14). But it's still good history. In the same way, there's not much statistical work done on Shakespeare, but you don't often hear scientists demanding that Shakespeare shouldn't be taught at universities. It's generally accepted that there is a value in the more intuitive work that happens in the humanities.

Second, it's difficult to see how the study of human sense-making can be truly scientific. Human reactions aren't the same thing as chemical reactions. A human being, faced with exactly the same set of stimuli twice in succession, will probably not react to them in an identical way twice in a row (the twentieth anniversary re-release of Steven Spielberg's film *ET* bombed, even though the film was the top-grossing film of all time for many years. The same film, released twice, can circulate in completely different ways.) The fact that human consciousness – the process of meaning-making – is involved necessarily alters the results of experiments into the human mind, as the philosopher of science Karl Popper argues:

> Large experiments in sociology are never experiments in the physical sense. They are made not to advance knowledge as such, but to achieve political success . . . They can never be repeated under precisely similar conditions since the conditions were changed by their first performance . . . [the social scientist] may be observing the principle which seems to ensure scientific objectivity: of telling the truth and nothing but the truth. But though he has told the truth, we can't say that he has observed scientific objectivity; for in making forecasts . . . he may have influenced those happenings in the direction that he personally preferred. (1972: 9, 15)

But, third, at an even more fundamental level it's also worth asking – is science really objective anyway? It's possible to argue that science is just one more culture that represents reality in particular ways. Feminist scientists, for example, have pointed out that the ways that science represents the world aren't just descriptions of the objective truth of how things *really* are: rather, scientific culture produces texts, like other texts, which favour particular ways of thinking about the world. For example, Bonnie B. Spanier examines the way that scientific descriptions of cells rely on cultural assumptions about gender roles. She explains how scientists describe the transfer of genetic material in the bacteria *E. coli*:

> One form of genetic transfer between two cells is the movement of a tiny circle of DNA called an F (for 'fertility') plasmid, with the aid of a bridge called a philus. The philus is a thin protuberance that grows out from the surface of the plasmid-containing cell (called F+) and attaches to a cell without a plasmid (called F-). In this process, the plasmid replicates, and one of the resulting two copies ends up in the second cell (now F+ because it contains an F plasmid) while the other copy remains in the original F+ cell. (Spanier, 1995: 56)

Spanier points out that the cell that grows the philus is called 'male' by scientists; while the other is called the 'female', even though there is no difference between them apart from the fact that one, temporarily, has this 'philus' growing out of it. Because one cell is passive in this process, it is called 'female', because the other one is active, it is called 'male'. As Spanier explains, these terms have no real relation to what we think of as being 'male' or 'female', these are just metaphors that take up a common prejudice within culture (men are active, particularly sexually; women are passive, particularly sexually) and apply it to the microworld that the scientists are studying, to help them make sense of it. A similar example is in descriptions of the behaviour of sperm and eggs in mammal fertilization. Spanier points out that in many ways the egg plays an extremely active part in the fertilization process, drawing in a sperm and absorbing it; and yet scientific representations of this process insistently describe the *active* male sperm penetrating the *passive* female egg.

Spanier's point isn't simply that this is bad science, or that it should be possible to describe these processes in ways that don't rely on any cultural preconceptions. Rather, her point is that all scientific data can only ever be described in language and that it must always be *interpreted* in order to be written, to be read, and to be understood. Science may aspire to complete objectivity and truth but it's just as much a part of culture as any other way of representing the world. Londa Schiebinger makes a similar point in relation to the history of the categories used in modern plant biology, developed by Carl Linnaeus in the eighteenth century. The taxonomy that Linnaeus developed for dividing plants into different types relied on counting the 'male' and 'female' elements of plants. Plants were divided into their different classes by counting the number of stamens (the 'male' parts); within these classes, plants could be placed into different orders by counting the number of pistils (the 'female' parts). There's no logical reason why the male parts should determine the most important division of the plants (into their general classes) or that the female parts should only matter at a subsidiary level. It was simply taken as obvious by the botanical scientists that the male elements were more important than the female (Schiebinger, 1993: 17).

The historian of science, Thomas Kuhn, says that these are not minor problems that will eventually be overcome. He claims that science will always be like this – a cultural representation of the world. He even points out that within the scientific community there isn't agreement on a single way to see the world: rather, science hosts a series of subcultures that have different ways of making sense of the world – different 'paradigms'. These are competing, and none of them is just 'the truth'. He describes research by scientist James K. Senior, who:

> hoped to learn something about what scientists took atomic theory to be, [and] asked a distinguished physicist and an eminent chemist whether a single atom of helium was or was not a molecule. Both answered without hesitation, but their answers were not the same. For the chemist the atom of helium was a molecule, because it behaved like one with respect to the kinetic theory of gasses. For the physicist, on the other hand, the helium atom was not a molecule because it displayed no molecular spectrum. Presumably both men were talking of the same particle, but they were viewing it through their own research training and practice. (Kuhn, 1970: 50)

Kuhn's historical account shows that scientific research always relies on the interpretation of texts: 'more than one theoretical construction can always be placed upon a given collection of data' (ibid.: 76). He points out that, like all of us, if scientists believe in a theory that they're testing then any contradictory evidence can be interpreted as proof that there's some other variable to be measured, whereas, of course, if they disbelieve the theory, then contradictory evidence can be taken as straightforward proof that the theory is wrong. When we read scientists' own accounts of what science is, and what makes particular kinds of knowledge 'scientific', we find that from the inside the practice of science looks very different from the crisp white coats and shiny surfaces of the Ponds Beauty Institute: 'knowing, even in the hardest sciences, is a risky, uncertain, subjective leap, even when it's most "objective"' (Rogers, 1968: 60)

> [for] Lancelot Whyte, the physicist . . . the truth value of a statement, even in science, could in the last analysis be evaluated by one criterion only: How deeply acquainted with the phenomenon, how non-defensive, how truly open to all facets of his experience, is the scientist who perceived the pattern? (ibid.: 67)

For, after all: 'Personal value judgements and informed beliefs are the basis on which one decides what is a sound or unsound direction in science; what evidence appears valid and what doesn't' (Coulson and Rogers, 1968: 173). Put this way, the process of producing scientific knowledge sounds a lot like the textual analysis I'm describing in this book: your research is valuable to the degree to which you're familiar with the area you're describing. Indeed, you could say that what is really surprising isn't how subjective textual analysis is: rather, what's surprising is that we think that science isn't subjective, as though scientists existed completely outside of the culture that they live in.

That's all very interesting. What's it got to do with textual analysis?

Scientific writing is a particular 'discourse', to use Foucault's term – a particular way of representing the world. It's the sense-making practice of a particular culture (scientists). But from a post-structuralist perspective it's not the only true, correct, accurate representation of the world. Forms of knowledge production which are more 'scientific' – using numbers to quantify data and using replicable forms of analysis – aren't more 'objective' than methodologies like textual analysis. It's true, though, that in our culture, numbers are often *thought* to be more truthful. As one statistician puts it: 'Some students of sociology have tended to worship the statistician as someone who, with the aid of his magical computing machine, can make almost any study "scientific"' (Blalock, 1972: 3). The common sense runs: statistics are facts, and facts are more real than description. 47 per cent of all people know that.

But statistical forms of information, like any other text, have to be interpreted in order to become meaningful. Indeed, that statement is a tautology – all I'm saying is that statistics have to be made mean ingful in order to become meaningful. Or, as an introduction to statistics for social scientists puts it: 'Statistics are a means of organizing, condensing and analyzing numerical data in ways that find order in chaos . . . [but t]he answers aren't in the printouts. They must be provided by the researcher' (Diekhoff, 1992: 4). Even numerical forms of information don't arrive from nowhere. They are always written by people – human beings with particular ways of seeing the world, who have asked particular questions, gathered particular kinds of data, and interpreted it in particular ways. There's no single correct way to gather data, or to interpret it – and no single correct question that can be asked in any area.

Take, for example, the statistics that represent a very real, everyday issue for many people, and for societies that claim to be humane: the fact of living in poverty. Now here is something, surely, that statistics can tell us something about. Either you are living in poverty, or you're not. That is a simple fact, a simple truth. Yes?

No. Consider the debate that raged in an Australian newspaper in 2002, arguing about how statistics about poverty should be gathered:

> A war of words has broken out between The Smith Family [a charity] and an independent research centre over claims the charity has exaggerated poverty levels in Australia.
> The Centre for Independent Studies [a right-wing research body] yesterday accused The Smith Family of misleading the public with a widely publicised study, which found poverty levels had risen during the 1990s from 11 per cent to 13 per cent – to the point where one in eight people were living in poverty in 2000. (Walker, 2002a: 3)

Some 13 per cent of people living in poverty. This is a statistic. It can be measured, and reproduced. It's a fact, it represents the reality of the situation.

Except, of course, it doesn't:

> The CIS claims the charity and its research partner, the National Centre for Social and Economic Modelling, deliberately chose a method of calculating poverty to fit their agenda. The CIS issued a report that showed 8 per cent, not 13 per cent, of the population lived in poverty and the income of poor families had risen by $38 per week during the decade. (ibid.: 3)

So is it 8 or 13 per cent of the population living in poverty? That's a big difference – about a million people. Someone's statistics are wrong.

Or rather, these are different ways of measuring poverty. There's no simple mistake in anybody's calculations – the opposing sides can't just check their calculators and agree on the correct number. They can't agree at all. Because the question here – as with all statistics – is about *what* to measure, and *how* to measure it. 'The Smith Family stood by its report released in November, saying it included twelve different measures, eleven of which showed poverty was on the increase. The charity said it chose a way of measuring poverty that encompassed the concept of social participation' (ibid.: 3).

As I argued in Chapter 1, people often defend their own interpretation of the social world as being just 'reality', that other people, for some mystifying reason, can't see. Because both sides in this struggle are laying claim – through the power of statistics – to represent the 'reality' of poverty, neither of them can admit that they are simply working with different ways of interpreting the world. Rather, they have to hang on to the belief that one must be right and one must be wrong. And so this debate rages on for several days, as the sides argue not just over how statistical data should be gathered, but what questions should be asked, and how the numbers should be interpreted – all in the name of deciding who will get to lay final claim to being able accurately to describe 'reality'. The government weighs in with its own interpretation of the situation (poverty isn't increasing, of course, Walker, 2002b: 6). Other welfare services contribute with their own definitions of what poverty is (Haslem, 2002: 5). The Smith Family comes back in to justify its definition of poverty (Henry, 2002: 8). Finally, a letter writer points out that the various parties all have their own perspectives on the issue:

> The Centre for Independent Studies, though It claims to be non-partisan, is clearly a right-wing think tank that produces research based on the political agenda of its directors . . . the majority of the board, including Hugh Morgan, are company directors whose boards have overwhelmingly supported conservative political parties and causes. The real question that their recent report raises is: Why does the Centre wish to argue that fewer people are in poverty? (Imber, 2002: 8)

Nobody argues that either the CIS, or The Smith Family, have got their maths wrong, or have made mistakes in data gathering or data processing. Rather, this debate is purely about the interpretation of statistics, and, the angry exchanges make clear, this is by far the most important part of the process.

If we're studying human sense-making, then at the some point in the process we have to rely on educated guesswork. Sometimes we can forget this, particularly when we're surrounded by people who claim to be able to understand and predict human behaviour in a reliable, scientific way. They're called economists, and we give them a lot of respect in Western cultures. But, like advertisers and public relations consultants, the practice of economics doesn't really match the claims. Economists rely on educated guesswork too.

Economics tries to predict human behaviour: will people buy things? What kind of things? Will they save? Will they stay at home or go out? Will they invest? and if so, in what companies? What kinds of behaviour by, and news about companies will influence the way in which people feel about them and behave towards them?, and so on. Ultimately, economics relies on a form of philosophy about human behaviour. And, despite its abstraction, its numbers, its orthodoxies and complex mathematical equations, economics turns out to be pretty poor at predicting human behaviour. As Paul Ormerod, a Professor of Economics, puts it:

The record of economics in understanding and forecasting the economy at the macro-level isn't especially impressive. Indeed, uncharitable writers might be inclined to describe it as appalling . . . the contrast between the actual scientific achievements of the discipline, and the confidence with which claims are made for it by its protagonists, is striking. (1994: 93)

Ormerod describes a survey published by an international body, the Organization for Economic Co-operation and Development, in June 1993:

The forecasting records of the two major publicly funded international bodies . . . the OECD itself and the IMF; and of national governments, were compared. For the major seven world economies, the forecasts for the next year ahead for output growth and inflation were examined. The benchmark used by the survey for comparison was a naïve projection that next year's growth or output or inflation would simply be equal to this year's. In other words, this benchmark required no knowledge of economics to produce . . . Over the 1987–1992 period, this extremely simple rule performed at least as well as the professional forecasters in projecting next year's economic growth rate. And in terms of inflation, the rule performed as well as the OECD and IMF, and slightly better than national governments. In other words, the combined might of the macro-economic models and the intellectual power of their operators . . . could not perform any better than the simplest possible rule which could be used to make a forecast. (Ormerod, 1994: 105)

Just because economics uses numerical methods of presenting its data about human behaviour doesn't make its research any more accurate in representing that behaviour: 'The theory of consumer behaviour hasn't fared well . . . both times the model was tested . . . it failed. The majority of test subjects didn't behave as economists predicted, instead behaving in a way that economists classified as "irrational"' (Keen, 2001: 16; see also www.debunking-economics. com).

In fact: 'Even fundamental concepts such as a downward sloping market demand and upward sloping market supply diagrams are invalid, more a matter of faith than empirically proven' (Millmow, 2001: 36). Economics uses statistics to present its educated guesses about human sense-making. Textual analysis doesn't. Neither can it predict human behaviour with certainty: just because economics uses numbers and iterable equations doesn't make it more true. Research on human behaviour relies on educated guesses – and it can be useful as long as the guesses are educated about how people make sense of the world. Whether it's presented as numbers or in descriptive language isn't really relevant, as this news story shows:

> Punters are better than pollsters [political researchers] at predicting the results of elections, a study of actual and forecast outcomes has found. Two academics who watched the odds offered by [bookies] Centrebet said: 'the betting market not only correctly forecast the election out-come, but it also provided very precise estimates of outcomes in a host of individual electorates . . . the press may have better served its readers by reporting betting odds than by conducting opinion polls . . . neither opinion polls nor economic models proved as sound as sportsbooks [bookies]. (Henderson, 2002: 2)

Bookies are no more scientific than are textual analysts, but the knowledge they produce (at least according to scientific methodologies used by the academics who researched this area) is more 'truthful' than the information produced by opinion pollsters who interviewed thousands of people and asked them how they intended to vote? Obviously, when you ask people a question, the answer you get is the answer they give when you ask them a question, it's not just the truth of what's really inside their heads.

Are numerical forms of textual analysis useful?

The most common form of quantitative textual analysis is called 'content analysis'. Content analysis breaks down the components of a text into units that you can then count. You decide on a series of categories and then you go through a number of texts deciding which ones fit into which categories.

For example, you might compare the coverage given to international news in different newspapers by counting the number of stories dealing with international news, the number of column inches devoted to each story, and perhaps the story's prominence within the paper (which page it appears on). For the most rigorous kinds of content analysis, the decision about which text fits into which category is determined by the presence or absence of keywords (if the story includes the word 'Clinton', then it fits into the category 'American politicians', for example) so that it's not only a methodology that produces numerical information, but it's also completely replicable – any researcher, given the same criteria and the same texts, will produce exactly the same results.

One advantage of content analysis is that it can provide a useful overview of how a particular issue is being represented in a large number of texts. For example, David Rowe analyses the representation of men's and women's sports in the Australian mass media.

> In the period 1980 to 1988, Australian newspaper coverage of women's sport rose from only 2 per cent of total sports reporting space to only 2.5 per cent, while in space devoted to sports results women's sport actually fell from 12 per cent to 8 per cent of all sports results, and there continued to be 12 times as many photographs of men's sports than of women's sports. Television coverage of women's sport is only 1.3 per cent of total sports time, compared with 56.8 per cent devoted to men's sport, 39.8 per cent shared and 2.1 per cent taken up by animals! (Rowe, 1991, quoted in Turner, 1997: 298)

Such figures provide useful information about the sexism of Australian sports coverage. They lead us to make an educated guess about the way in which sports viewers make sense of gender and sport (women's sport is less interesting and important than men's sport). Similarly, Graeme Turner reports:

> Groups of my students have prepared content analyses which compare the international political coverage of the three Australian commercial television networks with that offered by [the state broadcaster] the ABC. Their initial operating assumption was that the ABC, with its reputation for quality news coverage and without the need to allow time for ads, would screen a significantly greater number of international political stories. The research did not often support this assumption. Even more alarmingly, for those who might think the ratings simply test the entertainment value of the news, the research showed that the ratings leader, Channel 9 in this case, actually showed more 'hard' news than any of its competitors – including the ABC. (Turner, 1997: 298–9)

Again, this kind of statistical information is useful for thinking about the sense-making practices of audiences (in this case, to guess that audiences for commercial media are interested in overseas news stories).

As well as pointing towards large-scale trends in representational systems, statistical forms of content analysis can also be useful for a researcher who wants to get involved in public debate, and change the ways that issues are being discussed in the media. Statistics have a greater perceived truth value. News media love statistics, and journalists are more likely to take up a story with numbers in it than one that doesn't (Bennett, 1992: 32).

But these advantages don't mean that the numerical information produced by contents analysis is somehow more truthful (or accurate, or objective) than the information produced by post-structuralist textual analysis. There's always an element of subjective guesswork in research about sense-making. In content analysis, this occurs when the questions for the project are chosen; when the texts decided on; when the categories that will be counted are designed; and, most importantly, in the interpretation that is made of these in the final report – content analysis rarely publishes lists of numbers with no commentary. The biggest difficulty with content analysis is precisely that its insistence on scientific rigour – replicability and numerical reporting – can mean that it produces information which is far removed from the likely practices of sense-making for any given text. The researcher might interpret a text in a way that is quite 'mad' to non-academics.

John Hartley and I performed a content analysis as part of a large-scale project on Black representation in Australia. One of the categories that we counted was 'Crime stories' – media items which linked Black Australians with crime. We found out that in one week in 1994, there were 109 items in this category in our survey of television and radio programmes, newspapers and magazines: 109 media items linked Black people with crime, in one week. But how useful is that information?

At the time, a Royal Commission into Aboriginal Deaths in Custody had been set up by the government to look at how Black Australians are treated in custody, and to investigate police prejudice in the way they were treated. There were 46 stories about this Commission in the week we analysed. These were stories about social justice, arguing that Black Australians still face prejudice. Take out these and only 63 stories about Black Australians and crime are left in the sample.

If you then take out stories about police relations, the possibility of Black law functioning alongside European law, stories about Black Australians as victims of crime, Aboriginal television presenters doing crime stories, stories about Aboriginal rehabilitation, and white-collar crime by Black Australians, you're left with 19 stories associating Black Australians with the kinds of crime that they we might expect stereotypical links with. The initial statistic that might seem to give a broad insight into the functioning of the media in relating Aboriginality with crime turns out to be, not simply imprecise, but actually misleading.

And if you look at each of these 19 stories in detail, each of them can still turn out to be surprising. For example, one of these stories is a front-page headline story in the regional newspaper the *Sunday Territorian*: 'N[orthern] T[erritory] faces waves of violence', warning about a possible outbreak of crime by Indigenous Australians (10 July

1994). The story warned that the next generation of Black youth might 'unleash an epidemic of violence previously unseen in the Territory'. Reading this headline, it would be easy to categorize it as 'white fear of Black crime'. But looking closer, the claim is made by a Black politician, Charles Perkins. Illustrated with Perkins' photograph, it was his warning that violence might emerge unless Aboriginal people were 'found jobs and their standard of living raised'. This wasn't really a crime story at all – it was about social justice. It could be argued that Perkins was playing into the hands of racists: however, his strategies as an Aboriginal politician should also be respected. He used the crime story genre tactically, in order to get front-page coverage for issues of Black social justice (see Hartley and McKee, 2000: 221).

So we could say that there are over one hundred stories about Black people and crime in this sample. But the higher the abstraction in the statistics, the less likely they will bear a strong relation to inter-pretations of individual texts that might be made by readers. As we try to get more and more precise about how these texts might actually be interpreted, we have to make more and more exceptions and refrain from making confident numerical assertions, until we end up doing textual analysis, and not content analysis. To study every story individually and try to work out likely readings makes it impossible to deal with such large numbers of stories. Content analysis and textual analysis are different methodologies that produce different kinds of information. Those different kinds of information can be used for different ends. Neither of them is the 'truth'.

Are there more scientific ways of analysing texts without using numbers?

Sometimes in the process of textual analysis it can be helpful to draw on the ideas of 'semiotics'. Developed by French linguist Ferdinand de Saussure (and, independently, by Charles Peirce in the USA), this methodology has actually been named the 'science of signs' by some practitioners, because it tries to standardize the process of meaning-making. Semiotics is interested in sense-making, which it calls 'signification'. Each text is broken down into the 'signs' – units of meaning – that make it up. This might be words, colours, movement, particular sounds, parts of images, and so on. The researcher then treats these individual signs like words in language, analysing how they are put together in texts.

The biggest advantage of semiotics is that it makes us stop and consider the various elements of the process of making meaning from a text – steps that we normally do automatically and easily. The terminology and categories employed by semiotics are less important than the fact that they make us consider each element of the text, and the ways in which it's likely to produce meaning. The following terms are useful for this reason:

> *Addresser*: when we interpret a text, we often look for clues about who the author is, the image that we construct of this person is the 'addresser' of the text (whether or not that is actually the person who created the text).
>
> *Addressee*: All texts include clues about who they are intended for, even if that is as simple as the language they are written in (English, French, Esperanto, computer jargon, academic jargon, everyday language), but also including assumed knowledge ('As we all know, you should never mix spots and stripes . . .'). The image we construct of who a text is aimed at is the 'addressee'. These concepts can be very useful as we think about questions of 'wedom' and 'theydom' (see Chapter 2), and the ways in which we make sense of other people.
>
> *Phatic functions*: Not all of the elements of texts are interpreted as information. Some 'signs' are there simply to reassure us of the kind of relationship that we have with the addresser. The most famous example of this is the way that we interpret the spoken text: 'How are you?' 'Fine. And you?' 'Fine.' For most English speakers, this isn't interpreted to mean that the speaker is actually doing fine (Thwaites et al., 1994). It's just a polite gesture to show that we're aware of the other person.

But even here, with this 'scientific' method of analysis, if two researchers are given the same text and asked to describe the likely interpretations of its various elements, they won't produce the same answer. This is largely because semiotics – as with the textual analysis I describe in this book – recognizes that much of the likely interpretation of a text depends on contextual information such as genre, wider discourses in culture and 'intertexts' (other relevant texts, see Chapter 4). These contextual sense-making practices are called 'codes' in semiotics, and, as with post-structuralist textual analysis, researchers will have different degrees of knowledge about genres, other relevant texts, and wider cultural contexts. Or they may simply be analysing the text in order to answer slightly different questions.

Case study

Alan McKee (1996), 'A kiss is just . . .', *Australian Journal of Communication*, 23(2): 51–72.

This article analyses six examples of man–man kissing from television programmes, in order to understand what they tell us about sexual citizenship in Western countries. The research was inspired by the work of political philosophers who suggest that in order to enjoy full citizenship of a country, it's not enough just to get the vote: there are all kinds of public participation that tell us that we belong to a community and we're part of its public life. Queer theorists in particular have pointed out that by allowing gay and lesbian expression only 'in the bedroom', queers are treated as second-class citizens without the rights of public expression that are taken for granted by others.

I had noticed already that it was rare to see gay men kissing in the media, particularly on the domestic medium of television where 'children might be watching'. But it was OK for heterosexual couples to kiss. I wanted to explore how this hypocrisy is managed by examining the extent to which men could kiss each other on television.

I could have performed a statistical content analysis. It's quite straightforward to measure whether characters kiss: their lips meet. I could have surveyed hundreds of hours of television programmes, and counted the number of times in which male characters kissed each other. This would certainly have been a valid way to explore this issue, and I'm sure that the results would have been compelling: they would have shown that gay characters get to kiss each other much less than straight characters do. But I didn't think that such research would tell us anything new. It would simply confirm what was already obvious: there are very few examples of gay men kissing on television. Anyone who consumes a lot of Western television would be able to tell you this without doing any research: we know that such instances are still shocking, that when they do happen, they still result in media reports and headline stories. Counting up the numbers would provide statistics that could be used for press releases and trying to intervene in the public debate (see Chapter 2). But it wouldn't really tell us anything that we didn't already know.

I was more interested in exploring another, related issue that had struck me in my television viewing, that even when gay male kissing *is* shown, programmes tend to represent it very differently from straight kissing. They use all kinds of strategies to make sure that the audience knows that what they're seeing is not *ordinary*. They rarely represent the kissing as something that is familiar. The specific question that interested me was: How do television programmes make gay kissing look strange? This was a question that could only be answered by detailed textual analysis of a number of case studies, in order to try to guess the likely interpretations that audiences would make of these representations. I chose six television moments where gay or male–male kissing became an issue, analysing the ways they were represented and the interpretations that audiences would be likely to make of them.

The choice of examples wasn't scientific: I didn't employ a research assistant to go through every single moment of television broadcast on every channel over a period of several years in order to pick out every possible example. Rather, I drew on some examples that I had already seen and been thinking about, and looked for others by tracking down programmes that I knew (from my research, my reading and simply from living in culture) had queer characters in them. I kept my eyes open as I watched television, scanned the newspapers and magazines, browsed the Internet, for other examples. What I came up with was not a representative sample. I don't claim to be able to provide a percentage breakdown of the ways in which gay kissing are represented. Rather, each of the examples chosen represents a different approach to representing man–man kissing. Taken together, I think I can spot a trend that runs through them.

I began by identifying what I thought was the standard way of representing (straight) kissing on television, and found one example of man–man kissing being represented in the same way. This involved two characters, played by men, putting their lips together, involving no special effects either visual or aural. A pretty encompassing description: I didn't want to get involved in debates about whether the characters themselves were 'stereotypes' or 'positive images'; about whether they were in a committed monogamous relationship or had never even asked each other's names. I wanted to keep it simple: the actual moment of representation of the kiss.

This is how we normally see kisses represented, and so I guessed that for most viewers this would seem like an 'ordinary' representation of kissing. We're not supposed to be amazed that two characters are kissing. We are supposed to see past the kiss itself to its other functions in the narrative – perhaps it's reaffirming the love that two characters feel for each other; perhaps it's starting them off on an affair, or revealing hidden feelings. But the very act of seeing the two sets of lips meeting – that in itself is not meant to be shocking. And yet – and this becomes the central theme of the research – although you can find hundreds of examples of such kissing on television every day – with 'straight' characters – it's very difficult to find even a single one that involves two men.

I found one example of men kissing like this. In 'Out', a 1995 episode of the Australian television medical drama *GP*, Dr Martin Dempsey – one of the five central and regular characters in the programme – becomes involved with a male patient. This is presented to viewers as thought it's the most ordinary thing in the world. The *mise en scène*, the editing, the narrative, all construct this liaison as unproblematic. After a few dates, the couple end up back at the doctor's place; after a short flirting scene, they kiss. The image of the doctor kissing his boyfriend is visually unexciting. This image, this kiss, is a familiar, banal image of television soap opera kissing. Whether or not the characters themselves were the same as straight characters (Did they mince? Were they effeminate? Did they have lots of casual sex?) didn't interest me, but I was interested that in this one programme, the meeting of men's lips was shown to viewers as something *ordinary*.

This was my test case: an example of gay male sexuality shown on television, allowed into the public sphere as if there were nothing wrong with that. Against it, I could compare other examples of men kissing men – examples that, it seemed to me, were functioned very differently. From my knowledge of how television genres and television representation work, it was clear that these other examples were making men kissing men into something far more shocking. The second kiss that I used was one that would have eluded content analysis simply because it doesn't exist. This is the case of Steven Carrington in the American soap opera *Dynasty* (1981– 89). Steven was one of the earliest regular, central gay characters in an American television programme (although he later experimented with bisexuality). He was represented as being openly gay. He even had boyfriends. But he never kissed them. There is nothing to analyse in this textual analysis, apart from a very obvious absence. While other characters kissed their lovers – and held hand with them, and woke up next to them wearing delicate negligees, sprawled in artistically ruffled silk sheets – Steven didn't. Once, a lover straightened his tie for him. Another time, they had a fist fight. These were the kinds of physical contact he was allowed. And in a programme like *Dynasty*, where sex was constant and relationships a major theme, this was obvious to viewers. Steven talked about his sexuality (Finch, 1986: 34). But he couldn't have sex. This was my first case study of how television treats man–man kissing – refusing altogether to show it, and (by placing a gay character in a programme that is otherwise obsessed with kissing and sex) thus drawing attention to the face that male–male kissing is not a suitable subject for television.

My third example was the way that *Melrose Place* (1992–99) represented sexuality. The 1994 season finale explicitly draws attention to the impossibility of men kissing men through a spectacular imaging of not-kissing. The show features a regular gay character: Matt (Doug Savant). Matt is a central character: part of the show's close-knit community, liked by most of the regulars, hated only by the bad guys (Kimberley). He has never had a stable relationship, but this isn't surprising: no-one on *Melrose Place* has ever had a stable relationship. He's been involved in a series of flings and brief encounters, but at the end of the 1994 season, he has his finest hour. It's Billy and Alison's wedding (this will not come off, as repressed memories will cause Alison to run away and become an alcoholic), and Matt has just met the best man. He smiles, enjoys some eye contact, and goes in for something a little more touchy-feely. Standing by the swimming pool in *Melrose Place*, in the public space which lies at the heart of this community and programme, as Billy watches from a window, Matt and the best man move towards each other to embrace and kiss . . .

In some ways, Matt is lucky. In this narrative, he does at least get to kiss a man. But as they move towards each other, the programme begins to break down. Matt and Rob's lips never actually touch. The visuals suddenly slip into slow motion, with an almost strobe-like effect. The camera cuts to Billy, back to Matt and Rob, back to Billy. Finally, the moment of the kiss itself is represented by a close-up of Billy's face. The structure of these shots constructs the actual moment of the kiss – the possibility of two men's lips meeting, never mind the exchange of tongues or saliva – as the most incredibly desirable sight, with reaction shots and techniques such as the camera track and slow-motion making clear that what is taking place is the build-up to some explosive climax. And yet that climax is never reached. No kiss can be shown. It exists, in the story. But it is un-seeable. You'll go blind if you look at that kind of thing.

A fourth kiss comes in *Star Trek: The Next Generation*, and again, it wouldn't be picked up by content analysis. In the episode 'The Outcast' – which is, according to the show's producers, '*The* gay episode . . . a gay rights story. It absolutely, specifically and outspokenly deals with gay issues' (Jeri Ryan, quoted in Tulloch and Jenkins, 1995: 255) – a male member of the starship's crew kisses an androgynous alien. While working with the folks from the Starship *Enterprise*, Soren, a member of the J'Naii, 'comes out' to Commander Will Riker; she has 'tendencies' to femalehood, she confesses, and is in love with Riker – both forbidden by this androgynous race. The two go on to have a short-lived affair; they kiss, and we see that kiss: long, lingering, gentle. The screen then faces to black; in Western filmmaking, a well-known code for 'and then they nipped off and shagged in the bushes'. Sadly, Soren is kidnapped by the gender-police and forced to undergo treatment that will make her androgynous once again. This is the gay tolerance story of *Star Trek*.

Here's the thing: Soren is played by a woman. This is 'absolutely, specifically' an image of gay kissing, and yet it shows a man kissing a woman. Yet again, the representation of men's lips meeting is impossible for television.

A fifth approach to representing male–male kissing finds the sitcom *Seinfeld* actually managing to get two men's lips together, but only so long as we know that both of them are straight, and that the programme tells the audience that it should interpret the sight of the kiss as a hysterically shocking one. In the episode 'The Kiss Hello', Kramer kisses Seinfeld. Of course, this isn't a gesture of affection. We know very well that both Jerry and Kramer are heterosexual; more than that, we know that Kramer is eccentric. On top of all this, we know that the theme of this episode is 'kissing'. Visually, the wild gesticulations of Jerry's outstretched arms as he's kissed show his shock at what is happening; the studio audience screams hysterically at the sight; and then George comes into the room and performs an elaborate double-take. All of these things tell an audience who understands sitcoms that seeing these men kiss is not normal. It's outrageous. It's even slightly hysterical.

The final example of a gay kiss that I analysed was taken from the mini-series *Tales of the City* (1994): in this, the presentation of the kiss was much closer to the 'ordinary' kissing of GP than the others discussed but it's still not shown to be part of everyday life. We certainly get to see Michael 'Mouse' Tolliver kissing his boyfriend as they roll around the bed together, but this in a programme (based on Armistead Maupin's novels) which is textually and contextually proclaimed as being distanced from reality. As a special event mini-series, broadcast on PBS, *Tales of the City* draws attention to the unreality of its subject matter, a particular type of unreality named nostalgia. Set in an apartment block which is run by a dope-growing transsexual, everyone in *Tales* is celebrating the 1970s in the way that only hindsight makes possible. Joining consciousness-raising groups, enjoying free love, mind-altering drugs and kaftans, the programme celebrates what is consciously unreal, displaying an impossible yearning for what has never been. It's in this space of nostalgia, and sandwiched between a straight woman in love with a black lesbian who is really white, a transsexual landlady and child pornographer, that a man may kiss another man – so long as they both have 1970s' sideburns.

The methodology of textual analysis is applied to each of these scenes in order to try to understand likely interpretations that audiences might make of them and from this, to discuss the ways in which it's currently possible, in Western culture, to represent gay male sexuality. I applied various kinds of contextual evidence to the task of making sense of these scenes. I used generic understandings of how television programmes work (it's normal for characters to kiss in soap operas – if they are not gay; when the studio audience to a sitcom screams and laughs hysterically, you know you are watching something outrageous). I drew on my knowledge of the logic of specific programmes (it's not unusual for characters on *Melrose Place* to be involved with serial killers; it is unusual for them not to be seen to kiss each other). I applied linked intertexts (the comments about *Star Trek* made by its producers, and circulated in its fan communities). I used knowledge about how culture works more generally (television is a domestic medium, and it's limited in what can be shown by what is considered in culture to be suitable for children to see). All these kinds of information are necessary before these scenes can be analysed. And working out how they are likely to be interpreted by viewers makes an underlying trend apparent: to see a man kissing a man, to see homosexuality not as an 'issue' that can be discussed, but as a way of life that people inhabit – this is not yet mainstream. It's not yet acceptable to see 'in front of the children'. This textual analysis shows that there are still important parts of the public sphere where – as the political philosophers who first got me interested in all this suggested – gay men and straight people are systematically treated in different ways; where gay men are told that they cannot be part of the public, or part of public life, while heterosexuals are eagerly encouraged to do so.

And this research could not have been done, this argument could not have been made, simply by using content analysis. There's no claim in my article that the instances I have discussed are representative. I haven't attempted to measure how many of the representations of gay kissing on television fit into each of the categories of representation I've discovered. But if I had just performed a content analysis, counting the number of gay kisses on screen, then several of my examples would have slipped under the radar: no kissing at all in *Dynasty*; no kissing on screen in *Melrose Place*; no kissing between man and man in *Star Trek: TNG*. The basis of this work is my own expertise, my own knowledge of the television system, my own familiarity with the culture about which I write. That cannot be replaced by a system of coded categories and a team of research assistants. Content analysis can be very useful, particularly in providing statistics that let us intervene in public debate. But it can't do everything, and there are very real limitations to what it can see.

And the main points again

1 Scientific knowledge is usually numerical and iterable. Textual analysis is not.
2 This does not mean that it is less truthful, objective or accurate – scientific knowledge is one way of representing the world, not the truth.
3 Numerical and iterable knowledge can be useful for providing large-scale overviews of sense-making practices, and for getting media attention for your research.
4 The knowledge produced by textual analysis can be useful for understanding more likely interpretations of particular texts, as long as the researcher has a detailed knowledge of the sense-making culture they're describing.

Questions and exercises

1 Read through a number of newspapers in the library. Find quotes by economists. To what extent do they acknowledge that they are relying on educated guesswork to make their predictions about human behaviour?
2 Go the webpage of your national bureau of statistics (for example, in the USA, go to http://www.census.gov/; in Australia, http://www.abs.gov.au/; in the UK http://www.statistics.gov.uk/). Look through the kinds of information that are gathered in this

snapshot of your society and make as detailed a list as you can of the kinds of information that are missing. What details about people's identities are missed out? What kinds of cultural practices can you not find any information on?

3   From a library, find a biography of a scientist (type in 'biography' and 'scientist' into the 'Keyword search' in the catalogue). Read it, and make notes about how the scientist's life and culture relate to her/his scientific work.

4   Collect 12 issues of a magazine (from the library, or from your own collection). Ask a friend to help you. Develop an appropriate question for the magazine (for example, if you're analysing *Cosmopolitan* you might ask: What do women want in life, according to *Cosmopolitan*? If you're analysing *Modern Ferret* you might ask: What kind of people are ferret owners, according to *Modern Ferret*?). When you have decided on the question, you and your friend should separately perform a content analysis of the issues of the magazine. Separately draw up a list of categories that you are going to put stories into, and then count the number of stories that fit into each one. When you've done it, look through each other's answers. Did you come up with the same categories? Did you put the same stories in the same categories? Are there any interpretations that your friend made that don't seem convincing to you? And vice versa.

5   In the library, find a book that includes some content analysis (again, try a keyword search. If you can't find anything else, then use John Hartley and Alan McKee (2000) *The Indigenous Public Sphere*, Oxford University Press). Identify one of the texts (newspaper story, etc.) that has been analysed in the content analysis, and find a copy of it for yourself in the library. Do you agree that the category it's been put in describes your interpretation of it? What elements of the text are missing from that analysis?

Textual analysis project

1   Write down some topics about culture and how people make sense of the world.

2   Focus your question to be more specific.

3   List the texts that are relevant to your question from your own experience.

4   Find more texts by doing research, both academic and popular.

5   Find relevant intertexts.

6   Gather the texts.

7   Analyse as many of the texts in the genre as you can, gaining some sense of the rules of how they work.

8   Gain as much sense as you can of the wider 'semiosphere' (the 'world of meaning', or cultural context) as you can (read newspapers, magazines, watch as much television, listen to as much music as you can) to discover how these texts might fit into the wider context.

9   Bear in mind that as you gain more sense of the contexts in which these texts work, you might have to return to texts, rethink your interpretations of them, and produce new guesses.

You may have started off your research on lad mags worried that they represent a new expression of men's power over women. As you read them, and gain a sense of the wider cultural context they're circulating in, you might start to see them differently. Watching *Men Behaving Badly*, you might feel that it presents a similar form of masculinity to many of the lad mags, that both this text and *FHM* present traditional forms of masculinity in a very ambivalent way, as though they are intensely proud of it and incredibly embarrassed about it, at the same time. You might want to revisit your question, as you find that there is no consistent position on masculinity across the magazines.

10   Write up your results, in a suitable form for the purpose you want them to serve.

If you want to pass a university subject, or get a higher degree, then a more scholarly form of writing is appropriate (see Davis and McKay, 1996). If you want to engage in public debate, maybe a magazine article drawing on your research would be more appropriate. If you want to try to get something done about an area of culture that you think needs changed, maybe a report that you could submit to a government department would be most appropriate. You now have the results of your endeav ours: an account of the way in which lad mags celebrate and mock traditional masculinity, in ways that don't give readers practical instructions about 'how to' behave in everyday life, but do offer ways of thinking about their own gender role in a culture where gender roles are complex and changing.

Is that it?

Just about. It's a short book, with modest ambitions: to explain the logic behind this kind of post-structuralist textual analysis, and to insist that it's only one possible methodology for gathering data about sense-making practices. To finish with, one final case study that draws together all of the concerns of this book. It's an analysis of a number of texts, which isn't trying to judge which one is the most 'accurate' representation of reality. It looks at a number of different interpretations of a text: it doesn't claim that one of them is the 'correct' interpretation. Nevertheless, it's a piece of writing that believes that culture really matters – for how people make sense of their own lives, and of other people's – and that some interpretations are more desirable than others for particular political ends. And it's an attempt to change the way consumers make sense of texts, not by publishing an academic article that says the masses are stupid, but by writing a cross-over academic/popular book that people might want to read.

Case study

Catharine Lumby (1997) 'Beyond the real woman', in her *Bad Girls: The Media, Sex and Feminism in the 90s*. St Leonards, NSW: Allen and Unwin, pp. 1–25.

Catharine Lumby is interested in the ways in which feminist thinking has affected the likely interpretations of texts in Western countries. She particularly wants to know how audiences are likely to make sense of representations of sexualized women, given that everyone has heard of 'stereotypes' and 'sexual objects' by now, and these concepts are part of our everyday lives. She analyses an advert for a jeweller's in Sydney, as well as a number of relevant intertexts such as letters to newspapers about the advert and comment about it in newspapers and magazines and by public figures. She also analyses feminist writing about the media generally – writing which now provides a common-sense context within which people talk about these issues.

The text at the centre of her analysis is a photograph, described as follows:

> A woman is sitting in a chair reading a book. She has showered and put on a satin nightgown ready for bed. Her lover, who has just arrived home late from a business appointment, comes up behind her and slips his hand inside the gown to fondle her breast. The gown falls off her shoulder. Aroused but keen to finish the last few sentences on the page before her, the woman begins touching herself through the clinging fabric while her eyes linger on the book. (1997: 1)

How might we interpret this image, Lumby asks, and why might it matter what interpretations are made of it?

She begins by presenting the interpretation of this advert that she thinks is most useful for a feminist like herself. She knows that it matters how women make sense of their bodies. In Western cultures we've now reached the point where a woman can say that she feels 'objectified' by the way she is treated in culture, and most people will understand what she means. Questions about how we feel about our bodies are on the agenda, and everyone knows that these issues matter.

With this in mind, Lumby looks for an interpretation of the photograph that she thinks would be useful for women, and might allow them to think about themselves and their bodies in more powerful ways (see Chapter 2). For her, the photograph shows a game of seduction in which both partners are powerful:

> It's a common enough portrait of sexual intimacy played out in different ways in millions of Australian homes daily. One partner expresses desire, the other savours the attention before reciprocating. The roles are easily reversed. A woman might bite her boyfriend's ear or kiss his neck to seduce him away from a late-night television show. She might slap her girlfriend's bare bottom with a hairbrush for that matter. The game of seduction is open to both genders and all sexualities. (ibid.: 1)

But, as Lumby points out, there is evidence that many people didn't interpret the advert in this way. Many interpretations were quite the opposite, in fact. Drawing on a number of letters to newspapers, she shows that many of the people who saw this advert interpreted it in quite a different way: not only as offensive, but as a direct, and very real, assault on them. This advert was interpreted as: 'derogatory and demeaning in the extreme' and 'blatantly insulting not just to women but to men' (ibid.: 3):

> It is the most offensive advertisement I have ever been subjected to. It conveys the dangerously misleading notion that women condone and enjoy being molested by men and that this behaviour is completely natural. It objectifies women, demeans women and advocates sexual harassment and abuse, which is absolutely unacceptable. I am disgusted by this advertisement and feel that printing it is yet another crime against women. (ibid.: 3)

'It is a most offensive advertisement having connotations of women as objects, property and entirely at the disposal of men' (ibid.: 5); 'the woman has become comparable to a watch, available to give pleasure to the man' (ibid.: 9); 'I find it blatantly sexist, and not the kind of thing one expects to find in one's morning paper' (ibid.: 13); and '[I]t degrades women' (ibid.: 18). The strength of this language makes clear the importance of sense-making practices: as in the comment of the first writer, who feels she was 'subjected' to the advert. It has real effects on these viewers: they are offended, they are insulted, they are made to feel degraded, as though they are objects, simply by seeing it.

Of course, as I insisted in Chapter 4, this isn't simply the reality of how these viewers interpreted this advert: Lumby examines these letters as 'texts' as well. We will never know exactly what happened in the mind of these letter writers when they saw the ad for the first time, or on subsequent times. But do know for certain, from these unprompted texts, that the women were upset by this advert: upset enough to write a complaint letter, which is not an everyday activity for most people. And we know how they made sense of their own anger – what discourses, words, languages and ways of thinking about the media and representation, they drew upon when articulating this complaint. This is the trace that we can read from these texts, these letters of complaint.

The elements of this particular 'feminist' interpretation of the advert include:

- The woman is not in a sexual relationship with this man.
- She is not interested in sex with this man.
- His attentions are unwanted.
- To show a woman engaged in a sexual act (even if not explicit) is demeaning.
- An image of a woman objectifies her (there is no similar concern for the man, even though his head has been cut off and he is reduced to an arm).

There is no textual evidence *demanding* this reading, as Lumby makes clear. How does this interpretation come to be so obvious?

Lumby suggests that this interpretation – not just of this ad, but of advertisements as a genre, and of images in the media more particularly – is offered as a 'feminist' one in yet other texts, for example, in opinion columns in newspaper, in articles in women's magazines, in television and radio commentary (ibid.: 3). Even government publications offer this way of making sense of such texts:

> For more than a decade, research has found that the portrayal of women in the media and in advertising is grossly insufficient and inappropriate . . . Where women are portrayed they are too often shown as unintelligent, or sexy . . .Too often women are depicted as sex objects or victims of sensationalised and often violent sex crimes. Sexist stereotyping of women persists in journalism and advertising. (Crowley, quoted in Lumby 1997: 4)

As I argued in Chapter 4, audiences are not idiots; like media researchers, they learn ideas and vocabulary for making sense of the world from public debates. Lumby shows that the language of this kind of feminist thinking about representation circulates in culture, and is precisely the kind of sense-making strategy taken up by the writers whose letters she is analysing.

Acknowledging the multiple possible interpretations of a text such as this one, Lumby agrees that there are ways of interpreting the advert that support this interpretation, suggesting the woman's passivity and making it offensive for women who see it:

> Like traditional fine-art nudes shown staring, self-absorbed into mirrors, the woman in the satin gown enhances the male onlooker's voyeuristic pleasure in her body by demurely averting her gaze towards the book. The fact that the man is standing, clothed and anonymous (because we can't see his face) can also be read as evidence that the woman is a vulnerable object of desire. (ibid.: 7–8)

But, as Lumby suggests, just because there are cultural codes in place that suggest this reading – and just because other texts encourage educated women to make such a reading, as a political stance – doesn't simply mean that this is the 'correct' interpretation of this text (see Chapter 3). Rather, there are elements of the text that could be interpreted in different ways: 'For one thing, the woman is reading a book – an activity she doesn't seem eager to hurl aside just because hubby's home from the office. For another, she's touching *herself* – behaviour that suggests there's a little more to their sexual relationship than penetration' (ibid.: 8).

And, finally, Lumby suggests just why it might matter what is done with this text. As feminist writing has insisted (and as I argued in Chapter 2), how we make sense of the world matters. It matters how we think of who we are, what identities might be available to us, how we should behave, treat others, and so on. For Lumby it is important how viewers might make sense of this text. Like many other cultural studies writers, she wants to make a difference in the world (see Chapter 2), and so, by attempting to intervene in this practice of sense-making, Lumby suggests that it would be politically useful to offer women ways of making sense of such representations that don't lower their 'self-esteem':

> Why teach women to read images in a way that makes them feel bad about themselves? Why not encourage them to make creative readings of images and to appropriate and reinvent female stereotypes to their own advantages? Continually stressing the patriarchal reading of an image that can be read in other ways is hardly empowering for women. In fact, it's a strategy which cedes awesome power to images and to the people who produce them and which denies the ability women demonstrate daily to use imagination, critical resistance and humour in negotiating images and life in general. (ibid.: 9)

For Lumby – and for me, as I argued in Chapter 2 – how we make sense of the world matters. It is not simply the case that we can wake up one morning and decide to see the world differently (although many of the self-help books about happiness that I mentioned in that chapter talk as though that were the case – it may indeed be a possibility for some readers). Changing sense-making practices is a necessarily consensual process, whose outcomes are not predictable and where change can take a long time. But just as feminist thinking itself has – as Lumby demonstrates – been very powerful in offering new sense-making practices for women to think about their bodies and the texts that represent them, so she hopes that now it can attempt to teach other ways of making sense of the world: ways that do not insist so strongly that whenever they are sexual, women are being objectified (see also Albury, 2002). She doesn't perform a large-scale content analysis to see how many adverts 'objectify' women. Instead, she analyses a small number of texts in detail, and suggests that the very category of 'objectification' is part of the problem (see Chapter 5). Why shouldn't women be able to enjoy their sexuality in public, if men are allowed to do so?

So in this analysis, the advertisement is a part of the 'archive of sense-making' of representations of women in the public sphere – an example of how it is possible to make sense of women, men, and the relations between them. And the letters from the complaining readers are not simply the truth of the interpretations – they are another set of texts, which are analysed in relation to the advertising text, to suggest what interpretations are being promoted in public, what the logic is behind these, and what advantages and disadvantages such interpretations have. And Lumby offers an alternative explanation of this advertisement, one which her book *Bad Girls* offers as a political act, attempting to make other interpretations possible.

So there you have it. A good example of post-structuralist textual analysis. Go out and try it yourself. Work hard, have fun, ask interesting questions.

Good luck.

Further reading

This book has been very short and it has very modest aims. There are lots of things that it hasn't told you: but there are many other good books in the world that can help to fill in some of these gaps.

The history of disciplines that use textual analysis

To learn about the history of Communications as a discipline, have a look at two complementary articles by Bill Bonney ([1983] 2001) and Helen Wilson (2001). For a useful introduction to the history of Cultural Studies, see John Hartley's *Short History of Cultural Studies* (2002a); Graeme Turner's *British Cultural Studies: An Introduction* (1996); or the 'Introduction' to Simon During's *The Cultural Studies Reader* (1999). To get some sense of the kind of work which has been brought under the gambit of media studies, David Lusted's *The Media Studies Book* (1991) is useful.

An overview of the current content of disciplines that use textual analysis

As well as the Lusted book above, Michael O'Shaughnessy's *Media and Society: An Introduction* (1999) provides a useful overview for those interested in what might be included in 'Media Studies'. Denis McQuail's *Mass Communication Theory: An Introduction* (1987) remains a standard text for understanding the kind of work that is commonly brought under the 'Communications' banner. For a sense of the ways in which Cultural Studies practitioners approach texts, Lawrence Grossberg, Cary Nelson and Paula Treichler have edited a collection simply called *Cultural Studies*, which includes essays from most of the major approaches (1992).

An introduction to key terms used in these areas

For an unrivalled, intelligent and comprehensive introduction to most of the terms you will need to practise Communications, Media or Cultural Studies, see Hartley et al. *Communication, Cultural and Media Studies: The Key Concepts* (2002).

A history of textual analysis Graeme Turner's chapter on 'Media texts and messages' (1997) provides a very useful overview of the way in which the kind of textual analysis described in this book would fit into the ongoing history of the methodology. John Hartley's *Short History of Cultural Studies* (2002) traces the various theoretical traditions which have brought us to the point where it was possible to write this book.

References

Abdela, Lesley (2001) 'So many male stupidities', the *Guardian*, 9 January: 20.

Adler, Peter S. (1987) 'Culture shock and the cross-cultural learning experience', in Lousie Fiber Luce and Elise C. Smith (eds), *Toward Internationalism: Readings in Cross-Cultural Communication*. Cambridge, MA: Newbury House Publishers, pp. 24–35.

Albury, Kath (2002) *Yes Means Yes: Getting Explicit about Heterosex*. Crows Nest, NSW: Allen & Unwin.

Allen, Robert C. (ed.) (1992) *Channels of Discourse Reassembled: Television and Contemporary Criticism*. Chapel Hill, NC: University of North Carolina Press.

Amnesty (2002) Amnesty International – About AI, http://web.amnesty.org/web/aboutai.nsf, accessed 8 May 2002.

Ang, Ien (1985) *Watching Dallas: Soap Opera and the Melodramatic Imagination*. London and New York: Methuen.

APA (2002) 'Answers to your questions about sexual orientation and homosexuality', APA [American Psychiatric Association] Online, http://www.apa.org/pubinfo/orient.html, accessed 5 May 2002.

Artel, Linda and Wengraf, Susan ([1978] 1990) 'Positive images: screening women's films', in Patricia Erens (ed.), *Issues in Feminist Film Criticism*. Bloomington and Indianapolis: Indiana University Press, pp. 9–12.

Avert (2002) *Worldwide Ages of Consent*, http://www.avert.org/aofconsent.htm, accessed 10 May 2002.

Balazs, Janos (1985) 'Disturbances and misunderstanding in the use of address forms in Hungarian', in Richard J. Brunt and Werner Enninger (eds), *Interdisciplinary Perspectives at Cross-Cultural Communication*. Aachen: Rader Verlag, pp. 163–72.

Bantick, Christopher (2001) 'Play it safe and it'll be orate on the night', the *Australian*, 12 December: 13.

Barnard, Ian (1999) 'Queer race', in Alan McKee (ed.), *(Anti)Queer*, special issue of *Social Semiotics* 9 (2): 199–212.

Barrow, John D. (1992) *Pi in the Sky: Counting, Thinking and Being*. London: Penguin Books.

Bartley, Paula (2001) 'Review of Lesley A. Hall, *Sex, Gender and Social Change in Britain Since 1880*, History in Focus: The Victorian Era', http://www.history.ac.uk/ihr/Focus/Victorians/bartleyPaula.html, accessed 5 May 2002.

Becker, Carol (1997) 'The artist as a public intellectual', in Henry A. Giroux with Patrick Shannon (eds), *Education and Cultural Studies: Towards a Performative Practice*. New York and London: Routledge, pp. 13–24.

Bennett, Tony (1992) 'Putting policy into Cultural Studies', in Lawrence Grossberg, Cary Nelson and Paula E. Treichler (eds), *Cultural Studies*. London and New York: Routledge, pp. 23–37.

Blalock, Hubert M. (1972) *Social Statistics*. 2nd edn. Tokyo: McGraw-Hill Kogakusha Ltd.

Bogle, Donald (1973) *Toms, Coons, Mulattoes, Mammies and Bucks: An Interpretive History of Blacks in American Film*. New York: Viking Press.

Bonney, Bill ([1983] 2001) 'Two approaches to communication', *Australian Journal of Communication*, 28 (2): 19–32.

Bordwell, David and Thompson, Kristin (1993) *Film Art: An Introduction*, 4th edn. New York: McGraw-Hill Inc.

Bordwell, David and Thompson, Kristin (1997) *Film Art: An Introduction*, 5th edn. New York: McGraw-Hill Inc.

Bourdieu, Pierre (1984) *Distinction: A Social Critique of the Judgement of Taste*. trans. Richard Nice. Cambridge, MA: Harvard University Press.

Bromley, David and Richardson, James (eds) (1980) *The Brainwashing/ Deprogramming Controversy*. New York: Edwin Miller.

Brook, Stephen (2002) 'Cheeky hosiery ad unleashes censure', the *Australian*, 8 April: 5.

Brooker, Will (2000) '1954: Censorship and queer readings', in W. Brooker, *Batman Unmasked: Analyzing a Cultural Icon*. London: Continuum, pp. 101–70.

Brown, Graham (1996) 'Sexuality: issues and risk taking behaviour amongst WA gay and bisexual male youth', unpublished manuscript, School of Health Promotion, Curtin University of Technology, Australia.

Brunt, Richard J. and Enninger, Werner (eds) (1985) *Interdisciplinary Perspectives at Cross-Cultural Communication*. Aachen: Rader Verlag.

Carlson, Richard (1997) *You Can be Happy, No Matter What: Five Principles for Keeping Life in Perspective*. Sydney: Bantam Books.

Cohen, Stanley (1972) *Folk Devils and Moral Panics: The Creation of the Mods and the Rockers*. London: MacGibbon and Kee.

Coren, Stanley and Stern Girgus, Joan (1978) *Seeing is Deceiving: The Psychology of Visual Illusions*. Hillsdale, NJ: Lawrence Erlbaum Associates.

Coulson, William R. and Rogers, Carl R. (eds) (1968) *Man and the Science of Man*. Columbus, OH: Charles E. Merrill Publishing Company.

Craig, JoAnn (1979) *Culture Shock: Singapore and Malaysia*. Singapore: Times Books International.

Cuff, E.C., Sharrock, W.W. and Francis, D.W. (1998) *Perspectives in Sociology*. 4th edn. London and New York: Routledge.

Cuthbertson, Ian (1999) 'To boldly go', The *Weekend Australian*, IT Section, 6–7 March: 3.

Darnton, Robert (1985) *The Great Cat Massacre and Other Episodes in French Cultural History*. London: Penguin.

Davis, Lloyd and McKay, Susan (1996) *Structures and Strategies: An Introduction to Academic Writing*. South Melbourne, Vic: Macmillan.

D'Emilio, John (1998) *Sexual Politics, Sexual Communities: The Making of*

Homosexual Minority in the United States 1940–1970, 2nd edn. Chicago and London: The University of Chicago Press.

Diekhoff, George (1992) *Statistics for the Social and Behavioural Sciences: Univariate, Bivariate and Multivariate*. Dubluque, IA: Wm C. Brown Publishers.

During, Simon (ed.) (1999) *The Cultural Studies Reader*, 2nd edn. London and New York: Routledge.

Dworkin, Andrea (1981) *Pornography: Men Possessing Women*. London: The Woman's Press.

Ellis, Blain (1977) *Life with Aunty: Forty Years at the ABC*. Sydney: Methuen.

Ellis, John (2000) *Seeing Things: Television in the Age of Uncertainty*. London and New York: I.B. Tauris Publishers.

EMA (2002) 'Environmental Media Awards: General Information', http://www.ema-online.org/awards_general.htm, accessed 29 January 2002.

Empire (2001) 'The Bare Necessities number 9: *Suspira*', December: 11.

Empire (2002a) 'The Bare Necessities number 10: *Rebel without a cause*', January: 13.

Empire (2002b) 'The Bare Necessities number 11: *Gone with the Wind*', February: 11.

Fausto-Sterling, Anne (2001) 'Two sexes are not enough', http://www.pbs.org/wgbh/nova/gender/fs.html, accessed 4 July 2002.

Finch, M. (1986) 'Sex and address in *Dynasty*', *Screen*, 27 (6): 24–43.

Foucault, Michel (1967) *Madness and Civilisation: A History of Insanity in the Age of Reason*, trans. Howard R. London: Tavistock.

Foucault, Michel (1984) 'What is an author?', in Paul Rabinow (ed.), *The Foucault Reader: An Introduction to Foucault's Thought*. London: Penguin Books, pp. 101–20.

Froman, Robert (1970) *Science, Art and Visual Illusions*. New York: Simon and Schuster.

Fuglesang, Andreas (1982) *About Understanding: Ideas and Observations on Cross-cultural Communication*. Uppsala, Sweden: Dag Hammarskjöld Foundation.

Gamson, Joshua (1998) *Freaks Talk Back: Tabloid Talk Shows and Sexual Nonconformity*. Chicago: University of Chicago Press.

Gannon, Martin J. and Newman, Karen L. (eds) (2002) *The Blackwell Handbook of Cross-Cultural Management*. Oxford: Blackwells Business.

Gauntlett, David (1998) 'Ten things wrong with the effects model', http://www.theory.org.uk/effects.htm, accessed 8 May 2002.

Gibson, Mark (2002) 'Re: book', email communication, 29 May 2002.

Gillespie, Marie (1995) *Television, Ethnicity and Cultural Change*. London: Routledge.

Giroux, Henry (2000) *Impure Acts: the Practical Politics of Cultural Studies*. New York and London: Routledge.

Goldfarb, Jeffery C. (1998) *Civility and Subversion: The Intellectual in Democratic Society*. Cambridge: Cambridge University Press.

Gripsrud, Jostein (1995) *The Dynasty Years: Hollywood Television and Critical Media Studies*. London: Comedia/Routledge.

Gross, David (2002) 'David Gross' class notes on husband battering', http://www.vix.com/men/battery/daveclass.html, accessed 5 April 2002.

Grossberg, Lawrence, Nelson, Cary and Treichler, Paula (eds) (1992) *Cultural Studies*. New York and London: Routledge.

Haddon, Alfred C. (1910) *History of Anthropology*. London: Watts & Co.

Halperin, David M. (1989) 'Sex before sexuality: pederasty, politics and power in Classical Athens', in George Chauncey Jr, Martin Dubermas and Martha Vicinus (eds), *Hidden From History: Reclaiming the Gay and Lesbian Past*. London: Penguin, pp. 37–53.

Hartley, John (1992) *The Politics of Pictures: The Creation of the Public in the Age of Popular Media*. London and New York: Routledge.

Hartley, John (1999) *Uses of Television*. London and New York: Routledge.

Hartley, John (2002a) *A Short History of Cultural Studies*. London: Sage.

Hartley, John (2002b) *Communication, Cultural and Media Studies: the Key Concepts*. London: Routledge.

Hartley, John and McKee, Alan (2000) *The Indigenous Public Sphere: The Reporting and Reception of Indigenous Issues in the Australian Media 1994–1997*. Oxford: Oxford University Press.

Haslem, Benjamin (2002) 'Access to life's joys a better gauge of status', the *Australian*, 18 January: 5.

Hebdige, Dick (1979) *Subculture: The Meaning of Style*. London: Methuen.

Henderson, Ian (2002) 'Punters' poll noses sharper than pundits', the *Australian*, 2 April: 2.

Hendon, Donald W., Angeles Hendon, Rebecca and Herbig, Paul (1996) *Cross-cultural Business Negotiations*. Westport, CT: Quorum.

Henry, Elaine (2002) 'Rich rise would have meant more to poor', the *Australian*, 18 January: 8.

Herdt, Gilbert (1989) 'Introduction: gay and lesbian youth, emergent identities and cultural scenes at home and abroad', in Gilbert Herdt (ed.), *Gay and Lesbian Youth*. New York and London: Haworth Press, pp. 1–42.

Hermes, Joke (1995) *Reading Women's Magazines: An Analysis of Everyday Media Use*. Cambridge: Polity Press.

Hodge, Bob and Tripp, David (1986) *Children and Television: A Semiotic Approach*. Cambridge: Polity Press.

Hopkins, Kenneth D. and Glass, Gene V. (1978) *Basic Statistics for the Behavioral Sciences*. Englewood Cliffs, NJ: Prentice-Hall Inc.

Huffine, C.L. (1991) 'Social and cultural risk factors for risk suicide', in L. Davidson and M. Linnoila (eds), *Risk Factors for Youth Suicide*. New York: Hemisphere, pp. 40–54.

Hur, Sonja Vegdahl and Hur, ben Seunghwa (1993) *Culture Shock: Korea*. Singapore: Times Books International.

Imber, David (2002) 'Rich rise would have meant more to poor', 18 January: 8.

Imdb (2002) *The Adventures of Priscilla, Queen of the Desert*, Internet Movie Database, http://us.imdb.com/Title?0109045, accessed 2 April 2002.

Irwin, Harry (1996) *Communicating with Asia: Understanding People and Customs*. St Leonards, NSW: Allen & Unwin.

Irwin, John Keith (1962) 'Surfers: a study of the growth of a deviant subculture'. MA thesis, University of California.

Jackson, Dominique (2002) 'Hey, this is the reel thing', the *Australian Media Guide*, 10–16 January: 22.

Jackson Jr, Earl (1995) *Strategies of Deviance: Studies in Gay Male Representation*. Bloomington, IND: Indiana University Press.

Jackson, Sally (2002) 'A unifying thread runs through Kazai's outfit', the *Weekend Australian*, 2–3 Feburary: 12.

Jenkins, Henry (1992) *Textual Poachers: Television Fans and Participatory Culture*. New York: Routledge.

Jenkins, Henry (1995) '"How many Starfleet officers does it take to change a lightbulb?" *Star Trek* at MIT', in John Tulloch and Henry Jenkins, *Science Fiction Audiences: Watching* Doctor Who *and* Star Trek. London and New York: Routledge, pp. 213–36.

Jhally, Sut and Lewis, Justin (1992) *Enlightened Racism: The Cosby Show, Audiences and the Myth of the American Dream*. Boulder, CO: Westview Press.

Keen, Steven (2001) 'Economics: from emperor to vassal?', *Australian Universities' Review*, 44 (1&2): 15–17.

Kelly, Paul (2002) 'Reading a nation's mind', the *Australian*, 14 March: 1, 6.

Kingsley, Hilary (1994) *The Bill: The First Ten Years*. London: Boxtree Limited.

Kitano, Harry H. (1969) *Japanese Americans: The Evolution of a Subculture*. Englewood Cliffs, NJ: Prentice-Hall.

Krauss, Lawrence M. (1998) *Beyond Star Trek: From Alien Invasions to the End of Time*. New York: HarperCollins.

Kuhn, Thomas (1970) *The Structure of Scientific Revolutions*, 2nd edn. Chicago: University of Chicago Press.

Lévi-Strauss, Claude (1969) *The Raw and the Cooked*. New York: Harper & Row.

Linton, Ralph (1936) *The Study of Man: An Introduction*. New York: D. Appleton-Century Co.

Loveday, Leo (1985) 'At cross-purposes: semiotic schism in Japanese-Western interaction', in Richard J. Brunt and Werner Enninger (eds), *Interdisciplinary Perspectives at Cross-Cultural Communication*. Aachen: Rader Verlag, pp. 31–64.

Lowry, Brian (1995) *The Truth is Out There: The Official Guide to The X-Files*. London: HarperCollins Publishers.

Lumby, Catharine (1997) 'Beyond the real woman', in Catharine Lumby, *Bad Girls: The Media, Sex and Feminism in the 90s*. St Leonards, NSW: Allen and Unwin, pp. 1–25.

Lusted, David (1991) *The Media Studies Book: A Guide for Teachers*. London and New York: Routledge.

Magee, Brian (1985) *Popper*. London: Fontana Press.

McGrory, Daniel and Lister, Sam (2001) 'UK Muslim warns of radical converts', the *Australian*, 28 December: 7.

McKee, Alan (1999) 'Researching the reception of Indigenous affairs in Australia', *Screen* 40/4: 451–3.

McKee, Alan (2000) 'Images of gay men in the media and the development of self-esteem', *Australian Journal of Communication*, 27 (2): 81–98.

McQuail, Dennis (1987) *Mass Communication Theory: An Introduction*. London: Sage.

McRobbie, Angela (1997) *Back to Reality: Social Experience and Cultural Studies*. Manchester: Manchester University Press.

Michaels, Eric (1988) 'Hollywood iconography: a Warlpiri reading', in Phillip Drummond and Richard Patterson (eds), *Television and its Audience: International Research Perspectives*. London: BFI Publishing, pp. 109–24.

Middleton, David and Edwards, Derek (1990) 'Introduction', in David Middleton and Derek Edwards (eds), *Collective Remembering*. London: Sage, pp. 1–22.

Millett, Kate (1970) *Sexual Politics*. New York: Doubleday.

Millmow, Alex (2001) 'Keenesian economics, anyone?', *Australian Universities' Review*, 44 (1&2): 35–6.

'Miserable millionaires' (2002) *New Weekly*, 25 February: 12–13.

Mohl, Lucy (2002) 'Florence of Arabia: review of *The Adventures of Priscilla, Queen of the Desert*', film.com, http://www.film.com/film-review/1993/9279/14/default-review.html, accessed 2 April 2002.

Morland, Kenneth J. (ed.) (1971) *The Not So Solid South: Anthropological Studies in a Regional Subculture*. Athens, GA: Southern Anthropological Society.

Morley, David (1980) *The Nationwide Audience: Structure and Decoding*. London: BFI.

Morris, Sid (2000) 'Quality of life trails growth', the *Australian*, 13 December: 5.

Nanda, Serena (1993) 'Hijras as neither man nor woman', in Henry Abelove, Michèle Aina Barale and David M. Halperin (eds), *The Lesbian and Gay Studies Reader*. New York and London: Routledge, pp. 542–52.

Nava, Mica (1997) 'Framing advertising: cultural analysis and the incrimination of visual texts', in Mica Nava, Andrew Blake, Iain MacRury and Barry Richards (eds), *Buy This Book! Studies in Advertising and Consumption*. London and New York: Routledge, pp. 34–50.

Onishi, Norimitsu (2001) 'On the scale of beauty, weight weighs heavily', *New York Times*, p. 4.

Ormerod, Paul (1994) *The Death of Economics*. London: Faber and Faber.

O'Shaughnessy, Michael (1999) *Media and Society: An Introduction*. Oxford: Oxford University Press.

O'Sullivan, Tim, Hartley, John, Fiske, John and Montgomery, Martin (1994) *Key Concepts in Communication and Cultural Studies*. New York and London: Routledge.

Parkins, Wendy (2001) 'Oprah Winfrey's Change Your Life TV and the spiritual everyday', in Wendy Parkins and Tara Brabazon (eds), *Serenity Now!* Special issue, *Continuum: Journal of Media and Cultural Studies*, 15 (2): 145–58.

Patrick, Colleen (1999) 'David E. Kelley', *Screentalk: The Journal of International Screenwriting*, http://www.screentalk.org/banff003.htm, accessed 4 April 2002.

Penley, Constance (1997) *NASA/Trek: Popular Science and Sex in America*. London and New York: Verso.

Popper, Karl (1972) *The Poverty of Historicism*. London: Routledge and Kegan Paul.

Powys (2002) Powys Digital History Project, http://multiweb.ruralwales.net/~history/history/rhaeadr/poor8.html, accessed 5 May 2002.

Praz, Mario (1951) *The Romantic Agony*, trans. Angus Davidson. London: Oxford University Press.

Pullan, Robert (1986) *Four Corners: Twenty-five Years*. Sydney: ABC Enterprises.

Reeves, Nicholas (1999) *The Power of Film Propaganda: Myth or Reality?* London and New York: Cassell.

Robinson, J.O. (1972) *The Psychology of Visual Illusion*. London: Hutchinson University Library.

Roces, Alfredo and Roces, Grace (1985) *Culture Shock: Philippines*. Singapore: Times Books International.

Rogers, Carl R. (1968) 'Some thoughts regarding the current presuppositions of the Behavioural Sciences', in William R. Coulson and Carl R. Rogers (eds), *Man and the Science of Man*. Columbus, OH: Charles E. Merrill Publishing Company, pp. 54–72.

Rosen, Marjorie (1975) *Popcorn Venus: Women, Movies and the American Dream*. London: Peter Owen.

Ross, Ysaiah (2002) 'Legal ethics on tv through Australian eyes', *Picturing Justice: The On-line Journal of Law and Popular Culture*, 2 April 2002, http://www.usfca.edu/pj/ethics-ross.htm, accessed 4 April 2002.

Rowe, David (1991) 'Sports and the media', *Metro*, 86: pp. 41–7.

Russo, Vito (1981) *The Celluloid Closet: Homosexuality in the Movies*. New York: Harper and Row.

Schiebinger, Londa (1993) *Nature's Body: Sexual Politics and the Making of Modern Science*. London: Pandora.

Schramm-Evans, Zoe (1995) *Making Out: The Book of Lesbian Sex and Sexuality*. London: Pandora.

Seiter, Ellen (1990) 'Making distinctions in TV audience research: case study of a troubling interview', *Cultural Studies*, 4 (1), January: 61–71.

Shattuc, Jane (1997) *The Talking Cure: TV Talk Shows and Women*. New York and London: Routledge.

Shirtgod (2002) 'No fat chicks' http://www.shirtgod.com/fat.html./.

Simon, Anne (1999) *The Real Science Behind* The X-Files: *Microbes, Meteorites and Mutants*. New York: Simon and Schuster.

Spanier, Bonnie (1995) *Im/Partial Science: Gender Ideology in Molecular Biology*. Bloomington and Indianapolis: Indiana University Press.

Stocking, George W. (1982) *Race, Culture and Evolution: Essays in the History of Anthropology*. Chicago and London: University of Chicago Press.

Szalay, Lorand B. and Fisher, Glen H. (1987) 'Communication overseas', in Lousie Fiber Luce and Elise C. Smith (eds), *Towards Internationalism: Readings in Cross-Cultural Communication*. Cambridge, MA: Newbury House Publishers, pp. 166–91.

Szubin, Adam, Jensen, Carl J. and Gregg, Rod (2000) 'Interacting with "cults"', *The FBI Law Enforcement Bulletin*, September, 69 (9): 16.

Thwaites, Tony, Davis, Lloyd and Mules, Warwick (1994) *Tools for Cultural Studies: An Introduction*. South Yarra: Macmillan.

Tulloch, John and Jenkins, Henry (1995) *Science Fiction Audiences*. London and New York: Routledge.

Turner, Barry (1971) *Exploring the Industrial Subculture*. London: Macmillan.

Turner, Graeme (1996) *British Cultural Studies*, 2nd edn. London and New York: Routledge.

Turner, Graeme (1997) 'Media texts and messages', in Stuart Cunningham and Graeme Turner (eds), *The Media in Australia: Industries, Texts, Audiences*. St Leonards, NSW: Allen & Unwin.

Tylor, Edward Burnett (1871) *Primitive Culture: Researches into the Development of Mythology, Philosophy, Religion, Language, Art and Custom*. London: Murray.

Walker, Vanessa (2002a) 'Charity "fudged" poverty rate', the *Australian*, 16 January: 3.

Walker, Vanessa (2002b) 'Poor getting richer, says Vandstone', the *Australian*, 17 January: 6.

Waters, Brent (1996) *Dying and Death: A Resource for Christian Reflection*. Cleveland, OH: United Church Press.

White, Matthew and Ali, Jaffer (1988) *The Official Prisoner Companion*. New York: Warner Books.

Whorf, Benjamin Lee (1956) *Language, Thought and Reality: Selected Writings of Benjamin Lee Whorf*. Cambridge, MA: The MIT Press.

Wild, David (1995a) *Friends: The Official Companion Book*. New York: Doubleday.

Wild, David (1995b) *The Official Melrose Place Companion*. New York: HarperCollins.

Wild, David (1998) *Seinfeld: The Totally Unauthorized Tribute*. Milsons Point, NSW: Random House Australia.

Wilson, Angela (2000) 'Unbridled innocence', the *Australian* Media Section 12 October: 18.

Wilson, Helen (2001) 'Towards a non-binary approach to communication', *Australian Journal of Communication*, 28 (2): 1–17.

Wilson, Tony (2001) 'On playfully becoming the "other": watching Oprah Winfrey on Malaysian Television', *International Journal of Cultural Studies*, 4 (1), March: 89–110.

Winters, Richard (2002) 'On target all the way', Internet Movie Database, http://us.imdb.com/CommentsShow?109045, accessed 2 April 2002.

Wotherspoon, Garry (1991) *City of the Plain: History of a Gay Subculture*. Sydney, NSW: Hale & Iremonger.

Yamada, Haru (1992) *American and Japanese Business Discourse: A Comparison of Interactional Styles*. Norwood, NJ: Ablex Publishing.

Index